Henry
Bumstead

and the World
of Hollywood
Art Direction

*For Judy, with all best
wishes,*

Henry Bumstead.

Henry
BUMS

TEAD

and the World of Hollywood Art Direction

Andrew Horton

University of Texas Press ⤙⤚ Austin

Requests for permission to reproduce material
from this work should be sent to Permissions,
University of Texas Press, P.O. Box 7819,
Austin, TX 78713-7819.

∞ The paper used in this book meets the
minimum requirements of ANSI/NISO Z39.48-1992 (R1997)
(Permanence of Paper).

Parts of several chapters in this book appeared in
the film journal *Cineaste* 26, no. 3 (summer 2001),
as "The World of Hollywood Art Design:
An Interview with Henry Bumstead."

Library of Congress
Cataloging-in-Publication Data
Horton, Andrew.
Henry Bumstead and the world of Hollywood art direction /
Andrew Horton. — 1st ed.
    p.   cm.
Includes bibliographical references and index.
ISBN 0-292-70519-0 (alk. paper)
1. Bumstead, Henry — Interviews.   2. Motion picture art
directors — United States — Interviews.   3. Motion pictures —
Art direction — United States — History.   I. Title.
PN1998.2.B86 H67 2003
791.43′025′092 — dc21
2002154612

TO PHIL & NATALIE

Contents

Acknowledgments

A huge thanks to Henry Bumstead and his loving wife, Lena, for being so gracious and cooperative in my nonstop demands over several years of work. And a special salute to their hospitality at their home in San Marino during our days of shared work. Much appreciation goes out to so many who contributed to this endeavor, including Clint Eastwood, George Roy Hill, Robert Crawford, Marion Dougherty, Paul Newman, Robert Redford, and Robert Mulligan. I must also nod to the Academy of Motion Pictures Library Archive, as well as the University of Oklahoma and Dean Paul Bell of the College of Arts and Sciences for providing research support and assistance, especially through the Jeanne Hoffman Smith Chair of Film and Video Studies, which I hold. Many have made useful suggestions throughout this project, including Harriet and Sam Robbins, Mark and Victoria Eaton, Joanna Rapf, Peter Langs, and John Belton. My loving wife, Odette, and enthusiastic children Philip, Sam, and Caroline have all been supportive and have enjoyed and learned much from knowing Bummy! Finally, a hearty salute to the fine encouragement at the University of Texas Press from Joanna Hitchcock, the director, and from my editor on this project, Jim Burr, humanities editor.

Henry Bumstead

and the World of Hollywood Art Direction

Introduction
"Not Everything You Draw Shows Up in the Shot!"

When I first went to Europe, I went to Paris on Little Boy
Lost *[1953]. It was incredible because I knew Paris from my
studio work as a draftsman! . . . I had created it many times
before in great detail—on paper and in actual sets.*
HENRY BUMSTEAD

Dear Bummy, You take the BS out of filmmaking!
CLINT EASTWOOD on Henry Bumstead's receiving the
Lifetime Achievement Award in 1998 from the Society of Motion
Picture and Television Art Directors Society

In early August 2000, Henry Bumstead, one of Hollywood's most celebrated art directors and production designers, walked on stage in Los Angeles at the Hollywood
Film Festival Awards ceremony to receive a special award
in production design for a lifetime of work. At age eighty-
five, "Bummy" had spent quite a week, for his eighty-seventh film—Clint
Eastwood's *Space Cowboys*—had just opened to strong reviews and equally
strong box office receipts. Bumstead could well afford to smile that week,
for few individuals have left such a legacy in Hollywood. As Clint Eastwood made clear in a comment the year before, "I hope Bummy will work
with me until I'm too old to work because I know HE will never be too
old!"[1]

This book is a study of Bumstead's career from 1937 to the present
and his remarkable body of work, involving more than one hundred films
(this number includes his early films as a draftsman and several television
films). In addition to this impressive number of films, he has won Academy
Awards for *To Kill a Mockingbird* (1962, dir. Robert Mulligan) and *The*

Sting (1973, dir. George Roy Hill) and received Academy Award nominations for *Vertigo* (1960, dir. Alfred Hitchcock) and *Unforgiven* (1992, dir. Clint Eastwood).

Beginning at Paramount in 1937, Bumstead worked under German-born art director Hans Dreier at the height of the Depression, which he describes this way: "I was making thirty-five dollars a week when my classmates from USC who became lawyers were making ten to twelve and a half a week. In those days we did everything on the lot, so it was great training!" He went on to work with some of Hollywood's most talented filmmakers, making four films with Alfred Hitchcock, eight with George Roy Hill, and nine with Clint Eastwood. But that's only the beginning. For Bumstead has designed sets for Martin Scorsese, Abraham Polonsky, Franklin Schaffner, Michael Curtiz, Cecil De Mille, John Farrow, Leslie Fenton, Mitchell Leisen, Arthur Lubin, Anthony Mann, Daniel Mann, Delbert Mann, George Marshall, David Miller, Robert Mulligan, Paul Newman, Panama and Frank, Nicholas Ray, Mark Robson, William Russell, Mark Sandrich, George Seaton, John Sturges, Norman Taurog, Hal Walker, and Billy Wilder.

In short, Bumstead's career bridges the "classical" age of Hollywood set design within studios and the more location-oriented style of filmmaking that took hold after the mid-1960s. To trace Bumstead's work is therefore to track the changes in the field of Hollywood art direction over the past sixty-three years. What follows in these pages is an effort to capture part of the rich carnival of talent and experience that has made Henry Bumstead, or "Bummy" (as everyone who knows him calls him and as I will also feel free to do as well), one of the legends in the world of Hollywood art directors.

I had yet another motive in putting together this book, and that was to help shed more attention on one of the most neglected areas of film production. I would offer my own experience as testimony to this fact: before meeting Henry Bumstead, even after writing a dozen books on film and filmmakers, I was not aware of the nature and scope of the world of the art director or production designer.

Before going further, I would like to share a few words about how this study came about. I first met Henry Bumstead on the set of *The World According to Garp* when I was writing a book about director George Roy Hill. It was exciting to follow the pre-production as Hill refined the script with screenwriter Steve Tesich and author John Irving. I enjoyed watching a good bit of the shooting in a New York studio as well as at nearby locations as Robin Williams, Glen Close, John Lithgow, and the rest of the cast became the characters they played in Garp's complicated life. But the most unexpected pleasure of that experience was getting to know Bummy. When I watched the scene in which the airplane crashes into the house that Garp is thinking of buying, I realized that art direction was a world I was only beginning to understand, and I knew that someday I would have to devote a book to Bummy. After all, how do you design a set that an actual airplane can crash into *safely* and have the pilot climb out without a scratch? On that chilly morning at an abandoned New Jersey airfield, I was fascinated—or, to be more precise, I was hooked.

This book is thus the product of my fascination with Henry Bumstead and the field of art direction and production design. In a real sense, Bumstead is not only the subject of this book but also a coauthor, for his stories about his own work are so telling that I have balanced each chapter with a section featuring his comments as well as my study of his craft.

A final note: the terms "production designer" and "art director" mean basically the same thing. The early "stars" of the field, such as Hans Dreier, Cedric Gibbons, Richard Day, and William Cameron Menzies, were called "art directors." But with *Gone with the Wind* and a special award for "production design" to William Cameron Menzies, the term "production design" became the guiding label. Several of the studies listed in the bibliography (such as Beverly Heisner's *Production Design in the Contemporary American Film* and Vincent LoBrutto's *By Design: Interviews with Film Production Designers*) reflect this title, which has applied for more than fifty years.

The union for these professionals began in 1937 as the Society of Motion Picture Art Directors. Then in 1957 it became the Society of Motion Picture and Television Art Directors. Very recently, however, the union shortened its name to the Art Directors Guild. According to Scott Roth, the executive director, there are currently more than nine hundred members, who represent art directors and production designers as well as assistant art directors. "Many come from a background in theater, but theater designers have their own union, as do set decorators," comments Roth (personal interview, September 2000).

The Oscar and screen credit label is still "production designer," however, and in screen credits "art director" refers to the production designer's assistant.

As we turn to the career and craft of Henry Bumstead, we do so with the wise words of Robert S. Sennett in our ears: "Any attempt to generalize the working habits and personality traits of the great art directors and production designers is likely to fail" (27).

Henry Bumstead was born March 17, 1915, in Ontario, California, the youngest of three children (a brother four years older and a sister eight years older). His father, Lloyd, ran a sporting goods store and his mother, Emma Langman, was a schoolteacher. Ontario was a sleepy orange grove town of 10,000 at that time, roughly thirty-five miles outside of Los Angeles, and Bummy clearly remembers the presence and smell of smudge pots used in cold weather to keep the orange trees from freezing.

He describes his father as "a great guy," 6′2″, who had very little schooling but was fluent in Spanish, which he had learned from spending years in Mexico with his father. His mother was born in Golita, California, north of Santa Barbara, of British parents. Her family owned a ranch in Golita, and she graduated from what is now UCLA.

Bummy inherited his father's build (as did his brother) and became captain of the high school football team, a track star, president of the student body, and valedictorian of his class. But from early childhood he had a burning ambition. "I wanted to be a cartoonist!" he remembers with a smile. "We had no cartoons at the movies, and no television, not even radio at first, but we had the Sunday papers with all of those wonderful cartoons!" And while most of his friends must have remembered him for his athletic and intellectual skills, he always enjoyed drawing.

He got straight A's in art at school and enjoyed simply copying cartoons to get the feel for drawing them. "Barney Google, Blondie, Gasoline Alley, Little Ab'ner, Mutt and Jeff, the Gumps, and all of those great cartoons. I loved them all!" he remembers. Then in his senior year he found himself being courted by an impressive list of universities with athletic scholarships. "I was looking at offers from Iowa, USC, the University of California, and somebody showed up at the house from the Naval Academy!"

But his final choice was USC, which was a football and track power in those days and which offered him a four-year scholarship. USC had two major additional advantages: it was close to home, and it had an outstand-

A horse that Bumstead drew when he was six. Courtesy of Henry Bumstead.

ing fine arts and architecture program. "God bless them," he says of USC. "If I had not gone to USC, I would probably never have become an art director in the film industry."

As a freshman, he played football but immediately found that it was difficult to maintain his standing in the architecture program and play sports because "in architecture, you had classes and workshops from morning till evening." The conflict was, in a sense, resolved when he badly injured his back in a football game and spent almost two weeks in the hospital. In later life this injury continued to bother him, leading to two back operations. Thus for his sophomore year he dropped football but continued to run hurdles in track until he tore a ligament in his left leg at the Long Beach Relays. Then he made a fateful decision: "I'm going to go for an education" rather than sports. He is very grateful that USC continued to honor his four-year scholarship even after he dropped out of sports.

It was then that Bumstead, nearing the end of his sophomore year, began an internship that he calls "my first big break" and that led to his Hollywood career. "At that time there were only about eighty art directors in Los Angeles. Now there are nearly eight hundred," Bummy remarks. John Harkrider, who had just finished *The Great Ziegfeld* at MGM, asked his assistant, Jack Martin Smith, a graduate of the USC School of Architec-

Bumstead (second from right) running hurdles at USC. Courtesy of Henry Bumstead.

ture, whether there were any good architecture students at USC. Smith answered, "Yes, there's Henry Bumstead." He was hired by Harkrider, who was by then at RKO.

So he started interning at RKO in the summer of 1935. Bummy makes it clear that drawing wasn't his only strength. "I tell you, I was very good at lettering. For instance, I used to do all the lettering for the university. I did the lettering for Dean Weatherhead, head of the College of Architecture. So I just fit right in at RKO and made a hit with Harkrider."

Then in the summer of his junior year he got a call from Jack Martin Smith, who was now at Universal with Harkrider. "One of my fraternity brothers was Vaughn Paul, Deanna Durbin's first husband. And Vaughn's father was in charge of the lot, so he kept telling me his dad would make an art director out of me, and I said, 'I don't know enough to be an art director.'" But Bummy learned fast, met the stars, and enjoyed his work immensely when he finally began working for the studios.

Meanwhile, he was working on the side for a well-known interior decorator, Paul Frankel. Frankel designed furniture for films and for individuals who wanted custom-made furniture. Frankel sold to most of the studios and came to highly regard young Bumstead's work. When Bummy graduated from USC the next year, Frankel offered him a job designing and building furniture and wanted him to take over the business when he retired.

Bumstead turned him down, however, saying he wanted to have a go at working in the movie business. At that point Frankel said, "Then I will introduce you to Hans Dreier at Paramount because they are better than the other studios at paying their bills on time." And the rest is history, detailed in this study.

In his personal life, Bumstead married Betty Martin in 1937, a marriage that lasted until 1983. They had four children: Bob was born in 1941, Ann in 1944, Marty in 1949, and Steven in 1952. In 1983 he married Lena Stivers, and they have lived in an attractive home in San Marino since that time. An avid golfer, Bummy has not been a joiner of organizations or causes beyond those of the Art Directors Guild and the Academy of Motion Pictures.

HOLLYWOOD ART DIRECTION UP CLOSE

Let us ask the obvious question that actually has a rather complex answer: what exactly is an art director? No one answer encapsulates the whole profession or job description. But Jack De Govia, whose credits as art director include *Die Hard*, *Speed*, *Bowfinger*, and *Volcano*, puts it well when he says that Hollywood art directors are "architects, alchemists, illusionists; the modest creators of Heaven or Hell on demand, Eden or Gomarrah or Bedford Falls to your specifications, and we'll have it furnished for you and the utilities turned on, but don't open that airplane door, for you'll run into the stage wall" (2).

In short, it is the art director who stands between the screenplay and the director of the film, turning the printed page into a place real or fanciful, constructed or found, and who does so for a price the producer can live with.

To focus on art direction as the major part of the filmmaking process that it is, furthermore, demands a particular frame of mind. As C. S. Tashiro notes in his groundbreaking study of production design, *Pretty Pictures*, "Film design works from the difference between the physical world as it exists and the requirements of a particular narrative" (xiv). On the one hand, if an art director is doing his or her job well, we as spectators are not consciously admiring the "look" as separate from the story unfolding and the characters involved. In this sense, any set that calls attention to itself as a set is most likely disrupting the narrative by pulling us momentarily out of the story. Thus, as Tashiro suggests, to discuss an art director's work is to explore the gap between the "physical world" and the cinematic story being told.

The skills needed to create the cinematic environments in which stories take place require the art director to be a jack-of-all-trades. Vincent Lo-Brutto comments, "Production designers utilize imagination and technique, illusion and reality, and apply discipline and financial restraint to enhance the script and the director's intent visually" (xiii). There is therefore no bachelor's degree in film design yet in place at any school or university in the United States, as Ward Preston has made clear. In *What an Art Director Does* (27), he playfully but accurately explains what such a curriculum should be if one were to appear:

First Year
    Evolution of the Motion Picture
    Music Appreciation, Philosophy
    History of Art, History of Architecture
    Architectural Drafting, Perspective Drawing
    Designing for Motion Pictures I
Second Year
    Introduction to Motion Picture Production
    History of Motion Picture Design
    Interior Decoration, Creative Writing
    Computer Drafting, Perspective Drawing
    Designing for Motion Pictures II
Third Year
    The Business of Motion Pictures
    Set Construction, Location Facilities
    Special Effects, Computerized Photo Effects
    Illustrating and Storyboarding
    Designing for Motion Pictures III
Fourth Year
    Budgeting and Breakdowns
    Computer Design and Electronic Media
    Designing for Motion Pictures IV

Except for computer work, the list above represents Henry Bumstead's expertise. Art director Ken Adam (*Dr. Strangelove, Goldfinger, Barry Lyndon,* and many James Bond films, such as *You Only Live Twice*) states the basic qualifications for the profession more succinctly. "The sketch is the all-important tool of the art designer," he says. "I think it is advisable for anybody who wants to be a production designer to be able to freehand sketch, to have an architectural understanding of space, and then learn all the tricks of the trade" (LoBrutto 46). Once more, this sounds like a direct description of Henry Bumstead's major talents.

I wish to introduce from the beginning a term from the recent critical tradition of production, architecture, and cinema that says much about the whole territory of film production design: "cineplastics." According to architect Robert Mallet-Stevens, writing in 1925, "It is undeniable that the cinema has a marked influence on modern architecture; in turn modern architecture brings its artistic side to the cinema" (Vidler 14). This cross-pollination of art, architecture, design, and cinema is truly "cineplastics" — or in Hollywood's terms, production design.

As I pointed out earlier in this chapter, production or art design has been an underdeveloped subject in cinema studies. LoBrutto, in his collection of interviews with production designers, notes, "A mysterious veil hangs over the magnitude of the production designer's role in the film-making process" (xi). Michael L. Stephens is even more emphatic on the lack of awareness of cinematic production design: "When it comes to public notice and acclaim, perhaps the most neglected of the cinematic crafts is that of art directors" (1). We are used to examining films according to who directed them, who starred in them, and even who wrote them. But very little attention has been paid to a critical aspect of filmmaking: how a film looks.

That lack of attention is explained, in part, by the skill of production designers: if they have done their job well, there is the psychological reality that the audience accepts the set or location as "real" within the story unfolding on screen. Thus the muddy street in *To Kill a Mockingbird* looks as if it were shot in the South and not in a Hollywood studio (which it was), and the entrance of the American prisoners into Dresden in *Slaughterhouse-Five* looks like "Dresden" before the firebombing of the city, even though the actual location of that shoot was Prague. As Tashiro comments, "Part of the designed image's power lies in the environmental unconscious it creates, in which objects seem to sit naturally, just there" (172).

Before taking a closer look at the various phases of Bumstead's career, let us hear from Bumstead himself on a number of issues related to his overall experience and vision.

You began work in 1937, but you first began to receive credit in 1948 with
Saigon, *starring Alan Ladd. Can you talk about how credits work for art*
directors?

Bumstead: What you have to know about the credits is that for some time, even after *Gone with the Wind*, the head of a studio art department got his name in front of yours even if he did almost no work on your film. So many of those early films that I deserved really full credit for listed Hans Dreier or Hal Pereira ahead of me. But finally that bubble was burst. For instance, Pereira had his name on *Vertigo*, but he never had one thing to do with the film or Hitch! And he also had his name on *The Man Who Knew Too Much* since he was head of the department, but again, he did nothing on the project. This was true at every studio. That was just the way it was. Of course, this caused a lot of resentment over the years.

The amount of detail in your sketches is amazing. Is everyone that detailed,
or are you special?

Bumstead: Those of us at Paramount did more detail work than those at some of the other studios. But also I was just brought up that way, to be aware of so many things, such as texture and aging, for instance. One day things were slow when I was a draftsman, and I was working on a Victorian baseboard, which was about fifteen inches high going around a room. I was adding some detail work, and Hans Dreier came up and looked at what I was doing and said, "Henry, is this for the shot in the film of the mouse running along the baseboard?" Of course, there was no such shot! And I realized right then that I was too fancy! Not everything you draw in a detailed piece shows up in a shot. So I simplified the baseboard.

How big a crew did you have working for and with you in the old days, and
how big a crew in more recent years?

Bumstead: Very few, then or now. Because Paramount had only eight or ten draftsmen, period. And MGM had forty! You see, most set drawings are done at a quarter inch to the foot, then to three-quarter inch, then to

Sketch from That Certain Feeling. *Courtesy of Henry Bumstead.*

full size. But at Paramount we worked at half inch. That is, a half inch to a foot scale, you see. And then we went from half inch to full size, skipping the intermediate drawings that MGM and others did. Of course, I've always been known for being able to work with very few people. In fact, I've probably been known to have the fewest people of anybody. For many years I never had an assistant. However, since 1960, we have usually had an assistant, so I selected an assistant who could draw. For me, it wouldn't be useful to have an assistant who couldn't draw. My assistant cleans up my rough sketches and then turns them over to a draftsman [now called "set designer"] to make working drawings for the construction department.

From the times I've watched you on the set, I've seen that when they are filming and everything is going well, you leave and are busy getting future sets ready, so you really don't watch much of the shooting. Is this correct?

Bumstead: Correct. I hardly ever watch the filming. I'm always "working ahead." My routine is usually to check with the director or his assistant in the morning, and if they give the okay, then I work all day on future sets. I usually try to check with them at night, at the end of the day, too. So that if they need something for the morning, I can have it ready for them.

Sketch from The Vagabond King. *Courtesy of Henry Bumstead.*

You should also have the title of location hunter as well as art designer.

Bumstead: Yes, I think looking for locations is lots of fun, especially if you find what you are looking for. I have acted sometimes, too. For instance, in Yugoslavia, on *A Time of Destiny*, I played a two-and-a-half-page scene with William Hurt and Timothy Hutton. I played the part of a colonel. The film was directed by Gregory Nava, who did *El Norte*. I was freelancing then, working for various studios. And we built sets in Zagreb, Yugoslavia, and Trieste, Italy, and then we returned to San Diego to complete the film. I liked the film even though it didn't do very well at the box office. My acting day began at six A.M. to get a hospital set in a Zagreb church ready for my interior scenes. At three P.M. I had to get into my colonel's uniform to do exterior shots. I returned to the church around six P.M., but my scenes were not filmed until after midnight. A very long day, indeed. So I think I will stick to art direction!

Did you have a very different feeling about working with black and white as opposed to color?

Bumstead: Painting sets for a black and white film was hard. I was doing *Little Boy Lost* in Paris. George Barnes, a great cameraman, was lighting Bing Crosby. Crosby was getting older then, and Barnes was using scrims, etc., to make Crosby look younger. Barnes said at that time that black and white was tougher than color. It was tougher for the art director than color, because you had to be very careful what colors you chose to help the cameraman with his lighting. Cameramen had to separate rooms and sets by light. But good black and white films are gorgeous.

You jokingly say that George Roy Hill and Clint Eastwood have both playfully said to you, "Bummy, you are trying to direct this picture!" Did you ever get the bug to direct a film?

Bumstead: (laughter) No, no! I've never wanted to do that. You know, I've had fun doing some second unit work on *Slaughterhouse-Five* and on *Slap Shot*. No, I've never had the bug to do that. I think I would know how to direct because I couldn't lay out a set if I didn't know all the action required for a scene. But whether I could get the performances out of people, that's another thing.

What about the Art Directors Guild in its various forms and titles over the years. Have you been an active member?

Bumstead: You have to belong, and although I've always made over scale in my pay, I do feel the guild helps members in many ways. I was very active in the union when I was at Paramount. Because I was the youngest—the "boy"—in the art department, they sent me to all the meetings! So I went for years. But in 1960 I had moved to Universal, and I've cut down on meetings since then. Mostly because of my age and being out of town. But they still honored me, for instance, with a lifetime achievement award in 1998, and they were nice to feature me at the Hollywood Film Festival Awards in August 2000. I thank them very much.

When you first started, were there ever many women in art and production design, and is it different now?

Bumstead: (laughs) In the old days, I think there were probably three or four women designers and decorators, and they were good. Now it's the opposite. I would bet there are maybe more women decorators than men. And there are many good women production designers today, too.

Do you ever get a script that you say you can't do for whatever reason?

Bumstead: No! You never do that! But I do remember when I was doing *Absolute Power* with Clint, we had a lot of work to do on that picture. The actual production had not started, so I told the production manager, "Look, if you give me everything I need, crew included, today, I can have the film ready on time, but if not, I don't think I can do it." That scared them! So my crew and I left for Baltimore the next day and began.

What is the secret to such a long career in a business that has chewed up a

Bummy and Clint Eastwood on the set of True Crime. *Photo by Sam Emerson. Copyright © 1999 by Warner Bros. Courtesy of Henry Bumstead.*

Bummy receiving an Oscar for The Sting *with set decorator Jim Payne (far left). Courtesy of Henry Bumstead.*

lot of talent very quickly? You have worked steadily and successfully for over sixty years.

Bumstead: I remember when I was making A *Gathering of Eagles*, a B-52 picture with Rock Hudson, and our technical advisor was an elderly four-star general. I asked his wife how her husband got so high up in the air force, and she answered with two words: "He lived!" Yes, he had survived World War II. And I thought that was marvelous, so I do relate that to my successes. I lived! I survived! I'm an old-timer. And I'm still around! That's why I get some awards.

What do your Oscars and Oscar nominations really mean to you and to those you know?

Bumstead: Well, I think they are like any other business—75 percent or 80 percent of those given are well deserved. I mean, take those big companies in America: not always does the right person become the CEO of General Motors or president of Time Warner, you know what I mean? But then there is that 25 percent that can depend on sentimentality more than merit. When I told Morgan Freeman he should have won an Oscar for *Driving Miss Daisy*, he said he thought what really counted was just the nomination by your peers. And that's how I feel, too. But winning the Oscar is something else. It's a dart game. You have a one-in-five chance if nominated, and not every member of the Academy knows about art direction. So in a sense you are lucky when you win.

What do you see as changes in the young art directors coming up in the industry today compared to those of your generation?

Bumstead: One of the changes is that many of the new members aren't required to draw and detail different styles of architecture like we had to do in the days of the studio system. That's because so much of what is done today is location shooting. When I did *Vagabond King*, I had to be able to do all the Gothic sets and details. It's a tough style that I learned in my years at Paramount. Nowadays they would probably go to a castle in Europe to shoot! We had to know all styles, but that's not required anymore; yet it helps. It's all changed. For instance, in the paint department, it's hard to find anyone who knows how to "age" a set correctly. There just aren't many interested in being painters anymore. But in the old days, you could work steady as an "ager," and that holds true today.

So much of Hollywood cinema today seems to depend on special effects rather than art direction. What is your feeling about computer graphics and special effects?

Bummy on the set of Big Whiskey for Unforgiven. *Courtesy of Henry Bumstead.*

Bumstead: *Space Cowboys* was my first film with Industrial Light and Magic and the kind of special effects they do. They did a wonderful job, so it does seem as if anything is possible these days! But I am glad I was able to work during the studio system. In those days you worked out effects with the studio effects department, as I had to do on *The Bridges at Toko-Ri.*

You have just finished Space Cowboys *and you are eighty-five years old. Is there anything you wish to say about your age and your work?*

Bumstead: Clint just turned seventy, and he asked me, "Bummy, how would you like to be seventy again?" And I said, "Clint, I'd settle for being eighty again!" He got a kick out of that. It's a wonderful life! I feel so fortunate to still be working at eighty-five, and I give thanks to all the talented people who worked with me and who make it all possible.

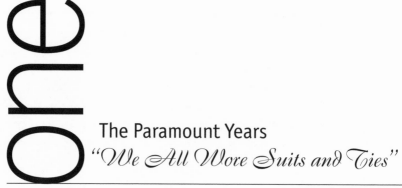

The Paramount Years
"We All Wore Suits and Ties"

Every picture is different.

HENRY BUMSTEAD

Bumstead joined Paramount Studios in 1937 and worked there until 1960, when he moved to Universal Studios. Paramount, one of the "Big Five" studios, had begun in 1914 as a film distribution company owned by W. W. Hodkinson and was to flourish in the years to come under the control of producer David Selznick (Schatz chap. 5). In fact, it became an extremely powerful studio during the silent period, working with the likes of Cecil De Mille on such spectacles as *The Ten Commandments* (1923).

Nineteen twenty-three was also the year that Hans Dreier arrived at Paramount from the famous German studios, UFA. By 1932 he had become head of the art department, a position that he held until his retirement in 1950. As Beverly Heisner notes in *Hollywood Art*, Dreier is in many ways best remembered for his work with two early star German directors who worked in Hollywood, Ernst Lubitsch, "for whom he developed the polished sets for sophisticated comedies, and Joseph Von Sternberg, for whom he designed the docks and city streets of the director's early crime films" (166). These films included Dreier's talented sets, which enhanced the passionate performances of Marlene Dietrich.

According to those who worked with and for him, Dreier was good at organizing production teams and encouraging new talent, but they also note that he set up a kind of militaristic hierarchy. Nevertheless, he was very much a "hands-on" head who was aware of every aspect of his teams' work. Boris Leven, one of his talented team members, put it this way: "Each morning Dreier would walk through the entire department, stopping at each desk, making comments on your sketches or on the film in pre-production" (ibid. 167).

Film historians have often commented that each studio had a certain "look" to its films. Dreier, however, discouraged this simplistic evaluation. He felt that "the art director is responsible for creating the reality of the backgrounds, against which the characters in the story move" (Naumberg 89). Yet Paramount did gain a reputation under Dreier for "sophistication, a polished and witty elegance different from the work of other studios" (Heisner, *Hollywood Art*, 170). Indeed, as one critic puts it, Dreier's style "has come to represent Classical Hollywood scenic design at its most elegant and refined" (Stephens 89). And Dreier, with a strong background in German expressionism at the UFA studios and an insistent eye for production detail, deserves much of the credit for providing an environment in which many older and younger art directors could thrive, including not only Henry Bumstead but such well-respected names as Roland Anderson, Robert Usher, Ernst Fegte, John Goodman, Earl Hedrick, Bob Odell, John Meehan, Robert Boyle, Walter Tyler, Bob Clathworthy, Tambi Larsen, and Albert Nozaki.

While Dreier was in charge of the art department, all of the films Bumstead designed at Paramount co-listed Dreier in the credits, as he was responsible for assigning art directors for each project. As Bummy and many other production designers working at that time have made clear, the head of the art department usually shared credit with the art director of the film. Thus, nine of Bumstead's films between 1948 and 1950 are listed on Dreier's filmography as well: *Saigon, The Sainted Sisters, My Friend Irma, Song of Surrender, Streets of Laredo, Top o' the Morning, No Man of Her Own, My Friend Irma Goes West,* and *The Furies.*

Upon Dreier's retirement, Hal Pereira took over as head of the art department and remained in that position until the closing down of the department in the late 1960s. Bumstead's last ten years at Paramount were under Pereira, who shared credit on all of Bummy's films during that period. These cross-listed credits with Bumstead in Pereira's filmography include *Dear Brat, Submarine Command, Sailor Beware, Rhubarb, Come Back, Little Sheba, That Certain Feeling, The Man Who Knew Too Much,* and *Vertigo.* Pereira, born in Chicago and educated at the University of Illi-

Bumstead at Paramount. Courtesy of Henry Bumstead.

nois, never had the high artistic reputation that Dreier has left behind, but he did apparently give those working for him relatively free rein on their projects. As Bumstead notes below, however, art director Roland Anderson was perhaps his greatest mentor.

BUMSTEAD ON HIS PARAMOUNT YEARS

Do you want to suggest some of your favorite films among the thirty-seven you labored on during those twenty-three years at Paramount?

Bumstead: That's never easy, but I'd have to say *Streets of Laredo, The Redhead and the Cowboy, The Furies* with Barbara Stanwyck, *Come Back, Little Sheba, Little Boy Lost,* and *The Bridges at Toko-Ri.*

What was it like to work at Paramount during the studio's "golden age"?

Bumstead: Paramount then was like a small town during the studio system. I knew everyone. They had talented employees, mostly under contract, in every branch of film—from producers, directors, cameramen, stars, and more. It was the old studio system, and I was under contract. They had talented people in every department. It was wonderful. That's why I like working with Clint Eastwood. We work with the same team on each film. I have worked steady through the years and never missed a day of work. So all I can say is I must have fooled them a long time! And they assigned me to good pictures and flew me first-class everywhere a project would take me.

You know, the person who saved my life, and I'm not ashamed to say it, was Norman Vincent Peale. His book, *The Power of Positive Thinking,* I used to read that all the time, because I was a very nervous person back then. Peale would tell you to write down the twelve things that bother you most, and you will find half never existed. That helped a lot. You see, I worked long hours and worked hard. On a typical day I showed up at six-thirty and got home about eight. We put in twelve-hour days regularly. The contract didn't say twelve hours—we just had to do the job. And in those days it wasn't much pay, but I didn't mind. I just loved working on films.

I was very lucky that from the beginning I worked mostly on big features. I've been blessed. I worked with good directors, good scripts, and good actors, and that has really helped a lot.

Your mentor at Paramount in many ways was the legendary Hans Dreier. Can you describe your work with him and his influence on you?

BUMSTEAD'S FILMS AT PARAMOUNT CREDITED
AS ART DIRECTOR, 1948–1960 (directors in parentheses)

1948   *Saigon** (Leslie Fenton)
        *The Sainted Sisters** (William Russell)
        *My Own True Love** (Compton Bennett)
1949   *Song of Surrender** (Mitchell Leisen)
        *Top o' the Morning** (David Miller)
        *My Friend Irma** (George Marshall)
        Streets of Laredo (Leslie Fenton)
1950   *The Furies* (Anthony Mann)
        No Man of Her Own (Mitchell Leisen)
        My Friend Irma Goes West (Hal Walker)
        The Goldbergs (Walter Hart)
        The Redhead and the Cowboy (Leslie Fenton)
1951   *Rhubarb* (Arthur Rubin)
        Sailor Beware (Hal Walker)
        Dear Brat (William Seiter)
        Submarine Command (John Farrow)
1952   *Aaron Slick from Punkin Crick* (Claude Benyon)
        Jumping Jacks (Norman Taurog)
        Come Back, Little Sheba (Daniel Mann)
1953   *The Stars Are Singing* (Norman Taurog)
        Little Boy Lost (George Seaton)
        Money from Home (George Marshall)
1954   *The Bridges at Toko-Ri* (Mark Robson)
        Knock on Wood (Panama and Frank)
1955   *The Man Who Knew Too Much* (Alfred Hitchcock)
        Run for Cover (Nicholas Ray)
        Lucy Gallant (Robert Parrish)
1956   *That Certain Feeling* (Panama and Frank)
        The Leather Saint (Alvin Ganzer)
        The Vagabond King (Michael Curtiz)
        Hollywood or Bust (Frank Tashlin)
1958   *I Married a Monster from Outer Space* (Gene Fowler Jr.)
        As Young As We Are (Bernard Girard)
        Vertigo (Alfred Hitchcock)
1959   *The Trap* (Norman Panama)
        The Hangman (Michael Curtiz)
1960   *The Bellboy* (Jerry Lewis)
        Cinderfella (Frank Tashlin)

*Credit shared with Hans Dreier.
For the remaining films, credit was shared with Hal Pereira.

Bumstead: There is a great lesson I learned from Hans. And this goes for Hitch, too. I don't remember which film, but we had a tight budget as usual. Well, I was designing a character's apartment, and to save money, I brought in some beautiful stock bookshelves. Hans stopped by while I was working and asked whose apartment this was supposed to be. So I told him. Hans said, looking at the bookcases, "Oh, he's a very learned man, isn't he?" — and walked out. Later I asked him what he meant, and he asked me if the character was the type who reads a lot of books. I said, "No." Hans smiled and said, "Then he really shouldn't have these bookcases!" So ever since, I have tried to do sets that fit the characters in the film. Hitchcock was the same way. Design for the character.

When I started at Paramount in the 1930s, we did everything on the lot, so it was great training. Hans Dreier always said we needed to study the architecture of London, Paris, New York, and Rome because so many films were set in those cities. When I first went to Europe, I went to Paris on *Little Boy Lost* [1953]. It was incredible because I *knew* Paris from my studio work as a draftsman! One of my first jobs for Hans was designing furniture for sets, and I did such a good job of it—because of my training with Phil Frankel—that it really sealed my future with him and Paramount.

I learned a lot from Hans. I was working on my first film as an art director, an Alan Ladd picture, *Saigon* [1948], and I had to create a waterfront bar in Saigon. While we were filming our first set, which was the waterfront bar, a technical advisor on the film came up to me and asked if I had designed the bar, and I said yes. He said he had lived in Saigon for many years and had never seen anything like our bar, so I returned to my office depressed. Dreier would come around once in the morning and once in the evening. So that morning Hans came up and asked what was wrong when he saw I was upset, and I explained. Hans said to go find this so-called expert and ask him if he had seen every single waterfront bar in Saigon. The tech advisor said, "No, but I saw most of them." Then Dreier told me to say, "Well, this one was just around the corner, you missed it!" I was never bothered by the tech advisor again. I've used that story often in my career. A great lesson I learned from Hans.

Who else influenced you at Paramount?

Bumstead: Roland Anderson, Cecil De Mille's favorite art director, took me under his wing and was really more of a mentor than Hans Dreier.[1]

I worked on a lot of De Mille films—*Union Pacific* [1939], *Reap the Wild Wind* [1942], and *The Story of Dr. Wassell* [1944]—as a draftsman. In fact, when I was drafted into the navy, even though I had two children at the time, De Mille wrote a letter, "To Whom It May Concern," explaining that I was a talented young man, and a hard worker, etc. I wish I had a Xerox of that letter!

But I had a great training on the job at Paramount. I worked, for instance, as a draftsman on all six of Bob Hope's "Road" movies: *Road to Singapore* [1940], *Road to Zanzibar* [1941], *Road to Morocco* [1942], *Road to Rio* [1947], *Road to Bali* [1952], and *Road to Hong Kong* [1962]. As a draftsman in those days, we did sketches, made models, and even got to supervise the construction of some sets with the art director's blessings. That was the studio system back then. And of course I got to work with Crosby and Hope! It took me seven years to become an "art director," but nowadays this generation wants to start on day one as art director on a film.

I did a lot of work as a draftsman on Billy Wilder's *Double Indemnity* [1944] and as Roland Anderson's assistant on Mark Sandrich's *Here Come the Waves* [1944]. I was sent to New York before World War II, my first trip to New York. What a thrill! I picked locations and took photos to help us build sets back at the studio.

Then World War II was on, and in 1945 I was drafted. I had two children then, Bob and Ann. With the help of Farciot Edouart, head of our Process Department at the studio, I got into the navy for fifteen months of active duty.

So being in the U.S. Navy, did you actually spend time at sea?

Bumstead: No. They sent me to the Naval Air Station in Bethesda, Maryland. I only saw action on ships as an art director on war pictures such as *Submarine Command* [1951], for which I made seventeen dives on location. That same year I also made *Sailor Beware* with Dean Martin and Jerry Lewis and *The Bridges at Toko-Ri*. Hal Wallis was the producer on *Sailor Beware*, which has a marvelous sequence as Lewis does a pantomime dance in a boxing ring. I remember he got a letter from Charlie Chaplin saying that was some of the greatest pantomime he ever saw. Jerry was just thrilled with that.

During those early Paramount days would you read the script and then make plans?

Bumstead: No, as a draftsman, the art director would give you the rough drawings of what he wanted, and you would turn them into one-half-inch-to-the-foot drawings with full-size details.

You have done sets for a lot of comedies. Was or is there any difference in preparing a set for comedy than for working on any other film genre? Do you have a "philosophy" of comedy?

Bumstead: No, I never had any theory, but after talking to film editors, I always felt what worked best in comedy were close angles. So if you get coverage in close angles, it's easier to edit. That is, it's easier to speed things up and get laughs.

I did six pictures with Dean Martin and Jerry Lewis, with Hal Wallis as producer.[2] He was one of the best producers I ever worked with. When you started a picture with him, everything was set up and ready to go: script, director, casting, simply everything. When he was at Warner Brothers, he did *Casablanca* and *Yankee Doodle* and many big films, and then he moved over to Paramount. But what I liked about him was that, even though he was watching the budget, if he thought the film needed a better set, he gave you the money. Or if he thought you were spending too much, he would take the money away from you. In *Sailor Beware*, for instance, as the submarine is going under water, Jerry Lewis stands there trying to sweep the water off the deck. It is very funny! I really enjoyed working with Hal Wallis.

Other comedies I enjoyed working on were films like *Aaron Slick from Punkin Crick* [1952]. That was with Dinah Shore and Alan Young and produced by George Seaton and Bill Perlberg. *Rhubarb* [1951] was pretty funny, too. It was about a cat that inherited a baseball team, directed by Arthur Lubin, who had done the Frances the Talking Mule pictures at Universal. *Rhubarb* was a cute script, but cats are very difficult to train. So we had six or seven cats, as I remember, to make it all work. And on *That Certain Feeling* [1956], I got to meet the famous cartoonist Al Capp because it was a film about Bob Hope playing a cartoonist. You can imagine what a thrill that was for me to talk to him since I had always wanted to be a cartoonist! *Knock on Wood* [1954] was a Danny Kaye comedy I enjoyed about Kaye as a ventriloquist [Gromak]. We shot a lot of that in England, but most of the film was shot on the Paramount lot.

You have done many westerns. What is it like to work on westerns from your point of view?

Bumstead: Oh, I love to do westerns! I've done so many—at least a dozen.

Sketch for Gromak's room in Knock on Wood. *Courtesy of Henry Bumstead.*

I like western and Victorian architecture. It's a lot of fun. Farmhouses, streets, jails, saloons—they are to my liking.

Let's get an idea of how you worked at Paramount by looking at one specific project. Come Back, Little Sheba *had been a hit Broadway play, written by William Inge, before it became a Paramount film in 1952, directed by Daniel Mann and starring Burt Lancaster and Shirley Booth, who won an Oscar for re-creating on screen her Broadway performance in this highly emotional drama. Did you see the play on stage? The film seems to have really just one set—the home of Lancaster and Booth. How did you develop the set?*

Bumstead: I didn't see the stage play, but I had a wonderful screenplay and Hal Wallis as producer. I found the exterior for the house in South Los Angeles. Then we built an interior set to match the exterior. We also matched the front porch so that we could shoot from the porch into the set. Also I made backings on location and had those installed on the set so that when scenes were shot looking out the windows or front door, it would have the look of that street.[3] In those days the backings were canvas and in black and white. They were called "Shipman backings" because of the company on Santa Monica Boulevard that made them for us. Of course, it helped that we had a great cameraman, James Wong Howe.[4] What a talent he was.

You know, he was a tiny man, and in those days we all wore suits and ties. And we would be on the set, the stage door would open, and in would come this tiny man with a beautiful suit on, and he was smoking

Sketch of the interior of the hotel in Lucy Gallant. *Courtesy of Henry Bumstead.*

a cigar. He looked like a kid in a suit. He was amazing. How lucky I was to work with him. What Howe could do shooting the Shipmans, as we would say, was truly amazing. I think the film had a very realistic look to it for this reason.

For Come Back, Little Sheba *as a sample Paramount film, how long did it take you to make a set?*

Bumstead: In those days, it was a few weeks to make drawings, and two or three weeks to construct the set and give the decorators time to dress it. We could work that fast because all the facilities were on the lot, and the decorators were so talented and wonderful.

We had a drafting room with draftsmen and illustrators. In those days I didn't have an assistant. Thus it was up to me to rough out drawings for the sets and give them to the draftsmen to make working [construction] drawings. This was the whole system that had developed under Hans Dreier. In other words, I gave the draftsmen complete rough drawings of what I wanted.

On a film like *Come Back, Little Sheba* I would have one or two draftsmen assigned to me, and a set decorator who would dress the set

Burt Lancaster in Come Back, Little Sheba.
Copyright © 1953 by Paramount Pictures Corporation.

with furniture, pictures, etc., and work with the prop man. So from the time we began work, we would have a set such as this one ready in about six weeks total. It varied by project, of course, but in general six weeks was fairly standard. And it was also standard to work overtime to get things done in those days, depending on the schedule, weather, sickness, and whether the company was filming faster than usual.

Were you paid for all the overtime work?

Bumstead: Before I became an art director, yes. But once I was an art director, no! I always laugh when I remember Hans Dreier calling me into his office and making me an art director, saying, "Congratulations, Henry. You are now an executive." Since that day, I went to work in the dark and came home in the dark.

Was Hans Dreier easy to work with?

Bumstead: Hans was very fair and good to work with. He came around twice a day, that was his way, and you always felt you could talk to him. He was very talented and professional. But Hans liked me for some reason. They say he had a son who passed away—I don't know if he saw me as a kind of son, but he was very good to me. And I liked his humor and criticisms. We were walking down the lot one day and Hans meets a producer who tells him what a wonderful job I had done on a recent film. Hans shrugs and says, "So what? He's a professional. That's his job, to be good!" That was Hans all the way! He wouldn't pat you on the back or flatter you, but he was fair. When he was being let go, he called me into his office and said, "Henry, the kind of pictures we're making now, you can do better than me. Now, you must go back to work since you are still on the payroll!" And that was it. The business had changed, and that was the last I ever saw him. You see, he started in film when so many of the directors were German and European, from Fritz Lang to Ernst Lubitsch. But by the 1950s, the directors and writers were Americans, and locations were becoming New York and other American spots rather than Europe and the "old country."

Speaking of the "old country," you worked with Billy Wilder on one film. What was he like to work with?

Bumstead: Wonderful. Well, even though I was a draftsman on *Double Indemnity*, I didn't really get to work with him as an art director until *The Front Page* [1974], which was at Universal. Funny, that picture never gets mentioned much in Wilder's work, but I think it's a good-looking film. He had such an eye for detail. In the newspaper office set we had, he wanted the name of the paper, THE CHICAGO TIMES, on the window so that when the light shone through, it would cast a shadow of the words on the pants of a character as he was standing in the room!

We had a good crew, and most of the film was shot in studio sets, but we did shoot some in San Francisco because it has so many buildings with big scale, like Chicago. Also we brought in a period train and shot the end of the film in the San Francisco station. But most of the film was shot in sets on stages and the back lot as well some scenes in old downtown Los Angeles.

What were some of the more unusual films you worked on?

Bumstead: *Dr. Cyclops* [1940]. It was directed by Ernest Schoedsack, who had co-directed *King Kong* in 1933. On *Cyclops* as a draftsman, I did a lot of the trick shots with the help of the cameraman and Schoedsack. I really learned a lot, so when Universal started the remake of *King Kong* in 1976, I was assigned as art director. We had started building sets, but it was canceled and MGM did the film. *Cyclops* was very interesting, however, and received an Academy Award nomination for the special effects, but did not receive the award.

Did you work on any films that you were not credited for at all?

Bumstead: Yes, a few. I did work on other films that I have no official credit on. You see, when an art director would get in a jam, we would be assigned to help out if we weren't too busy. For instance, I helped out on *Whispering Smith* [1948]. Walter Tyler was the art director, and I did second unit work on location. I also helped on Billy Wilder's *Sabrina*. Walter Tyler was the art director and Mac Johnson was the art director on Marlon Brando's *One Eyed Jacks* in Monterey, California, which I also helped out on.

"I NEVER HAD AN ASSISTANT": CLOSE-UP ON FOUR OF BUMSTEAD'S PARAMOUNT FILMS

I have chosen to represent Bumstead's ability to work on a wide range of materials by selecting four films from four different genres that he was assigned to during his Paramount years, with selected sketches to illustrate his designs.[5] One point worth making here is how much of the project was Bumstead's sole responsibility. Of course, he had a team that he would work with, which included the set decorator and a draftsman. Then there were the various construction folk and painters who were pulled in as needed. But surprisingly Bumstead makes it clear that "I never had an assistant until I was working on George Roy Hill's *Slaughterhouse-Five* in 1972." Like many details of his profession, it's difficult for those on the outside to imagine how one person could do all he and other production designers were expected to do. Working many days from six A.M. to long past six P.M. for so many years, with not a day missed for illness, Henry Bumstead supervised and planned the production of sets for film after film.

Designing Comedy: *My Friend Irma*

My Friend Irma (1949); *directed by George Marshall; produced by Hal Wallis; written by Cy Howard and Park Levy from the radio show by Cy Howard; cinematography by Leo Tover. Cast: Marie Wilson, John Lund, Diana Lynn, and introducing Dean Martin and Jerry Lewis in their first film.*

Originally a popular CBS radio show, this spirited comedy follows dumb blonde Wilson as Irma and her best friend, Diana Lynn. Comedy erupts as they run into Martin and Lewis, a struggling "new talent" duo trying to become a nightclub act, all set in New York City. Narrator/character Diana Lynn says late in the film, "Anything can happen if you live with my friend Irma," and for a comic hour and a half, of course, "anything" does become "everything," much to our amusement. *Irma* was directed with a flair for comedy by George Marshall, who had by this time already directed Laurel and Hardy, W. C. Fields, Bob Hope, and others. Bummy describes Marshall as "a sweetheart" who listened to everyone quietly, professionally, and politely. "I remember he walked onto one of my sets and studied it and then said, 'Well, I didn't think of that door being over there, but maybe it will work just as well where it is,' instead of saying, 'Change it!'"

This was a Hal Wallis production, and Bumstead has expressed admiration for the way Wallis ran a "hands-on" production, watching the dailies every day to make suggestions, changes, and improvements. On this project his sense of taking chances could be seen in signing up Martin and Lewis for their first film. According to Lewis's biographer, Shawn Levy, "Wallis had made a specialty of scouting fresh talent and securing it for the long run: he kept Kirk Douglas, Burt Lancaster, and Charlton Heston working in low-budget movies until they made a name for themselves" (102).

An overall note on comedy and set design is perhaps helpful before taking a closer look at Bummy's work. Bumstead has been a firm believer that a set per se in most comedies is not meant to be funny. The characters carry the laughs. And this is in large part because most of the comedies he worked on, such as *My Friend Irma*, are grounded in "realism." That is, New York is supposed to look like New York in this story so that we laugh thinking of characters like Irma, not to mention Jerry Lewis, acting the way they do in situations we can all recognize. Thus Bumstead's charge was to go for "realism" rather than "comic" in terms of set design.

This would not be true for what I have called "anarchistic comedy"— those comedies of the Marx Brothers, Monty Python, and others in which the whole point is to push far beyond realism into absurd exaggeration and distortion for humor (Horton, *Comedy/Cinema/Theory*, 10). Taking all of this into consideration, however, there is a general tendency for comedies to be brightly lit. Thus note how many of the sets mentioned below do "radiate" this quality.

Imagine the pace of work for Bumstead and his team as they completed *Irma*, with more than a dozen full sets, in addition to three other features in 1949 alone. Once more, let me emphasize how different such a studio-produced film was from most of today's films, which make extensive use of location shooting. *Captain Corelli's Mandolin* (2001), for instance, even adds a line in its credits that the film was completely shot on the Greek island of Cephalonia, where the action of this World War II story takes place. I will discuss Bumstead's "location" films too, but here the focus is on working within the studio in California. That said, let's review nine of the sets on this project and the complexity and special features of each.

Street Scene of New York City (Opening and Closing Scenes)

The opening and closing shot has Irma strutting down a busy New York City street that is under construction. The comic point is that Irma is so absorbed in her own world that she is oblivious to the BEWARE/CONSTRUC-TION signs and drops down a hole in the pavement where the street is being repaired. This set looks so like New York that anyone today would swear the scenes were shot on location. But Bummy explains that Hans Dreier had created a great New York street set that was used for many films—with alterations, of course. "It had scale," he comments, meaning that it seemed more realistic than some other studio New York sets.

After a recent viewing of the film, Bumstead observed that a number of the sets for *Irma*, such as those for the rich man's home and perhaps for the nightclubs, may well have been used for other films of the time since Hal Wallis "would not have spent so much money as the sets appear to have cost on one film alone!" Certainly such "recycling" of sets was a creative and thrifty part of the studio system's method for so many years. Many have commented, for instance, that the elaborate set for the Babylon sequences in D. W. Griffith's *Intolerance* (1916) was reused in dozens of films afterward (Ettedgui 8).

Irma's Apartment (Interior and Exterior)

Late 1940s New York. The apartment of these two twentysomething girlfriends is both cluttered and spacious—spacious in the sense that today a remake of *Irma* would require Bumstead to design an apartment the size of a large closet! And the delightful clutter of beds, too much furniture, and "stuff" is done on purpose. Bumstead explains, "In those days you would assume each girl was either given or inherited furniture and things they felt they had to hold on to!" Comedy thrives on "bright," as many comedians point out, and this set is full of light.

The actual set is obviously under the eye of the art director. But what of all of the objects and furniture therein? Again, Bumstead had final approval (with Hans Dreier looking over his shoulder!), but the set decorator would confer with Bummy and carry out this area of work. Thus, in conjunction with the set decorator, Bumstead approved the idea of "misplaced" objects—Irma's coffee pot kept in the fridge, the fry pan in the radio cabinet—that comically suggest Irma's confused lifestyle.

A New York Diner (Dining Area and Kitchen)
We first meet Martin and Lewis in the brightly lit kitchen of a New York diner, as Jerry squeezes oranges to make juice in his screen debut. The set is almost abstractly simple to help draw full attention to Lewis, and it succeeds. We can't help but focus on this wiry guy with such a strange voice and such strangely twisted hands. In contrast, the dining area has that art nouveau look of classic American diners, and, in the spirit of comedy, is also brightly lit.

A Fancy Businessman's Office
Irma's roommate works for a serious businessman, and his dark, wood-paneled office reflects such sobriety. Attention to detail in props includes a fancy model ship behind the boss near the desk, a detail that Bumstead takes pride in having suggested for the scene ("I just felt he was the kind of guy who might collect model ships!"). The point here is that such a detail was not in the script. This and thousands of other details over the years in Bumstead's films (and those of any good art director) are the product of a creative collaboration in bringing the set to life as part of the character of the actual protagonists on screen.

The Gypsy Tea Room Restaurant/Dance Club
Here Bumstead went for a bistro look that feels close and intimate as dining tables and performance area are set in a rather small area. It is here that Martin and Lewis "perform" and are discovered.

Apartment Rooftop with View of New York
One set is a New York rooftop apartment with rear projection of a New York night skyline surrounding it. To Bumstead's credit, this studio-built location has a very authentic look to it.

Modern Nightclub: Casino Gardens (Interior and Exterior)

Casino Gardens is the upscale "big-time" nightclub where Dean Martin finally gets his big chance while Jerry Lewis is relegated to making a mess of parking cars in a huge parking lot. Again, Bumstead manages to combine a sense of spaciousness and bright luminosity for the dining and dance band interior, contrasting with the crowded and darkly lit parking lot that Lewis works in, all done on the lot.

Home of a Rich Man and Home of a Rich Woman

Irma contrasts the lower-middle-class working world of Irma and her roommate with the lives of the very rich. These two "wealthy" sets immediately establish the "upstairs/downstairs" social contrasts between our main characters and those they have come to know.

Under the Brooklyn Bridge

Like the rooftop view of New York, this night scene with the Brooklyn Bridge in the background is so well set up that we feel we are on location, but Bumstead and crew have once more created such a feeling on a California stage with rear projection of the Brooklyn Bridge.

Designing Comedy: *Hollywood or Bust*

Bumstead went on to work on a handful of other Jerry Lewis films, including *Sailor Beware* (1951), *Jumping Jacks* (1952), *Hollywood or Bust* (1956), *The Bellboy*, and *Cinderfella* (both 1960). Bumstead used his talents well on all of Lewis's films, even when the scripts were not as convincing as the sets.

Such was the case with the last Martin and Lewis film, *Hollywood or Bust*, directed by the talented Frank Tashlin, whose credits included such hits as *Son of Paleface*, *The Girl Can't Help It*, and *Disorderly Orderly*, but with a spotty script by Erna Lazarus. The main problem, however, on the set of this simple tale—in which Martin and Lewis win a car on the East Coast and drive across America, headed for Hollywood—was that Martin and Lewis were ready to split. According to those on the set, Jerry worked hard to sabotage every scene because of his anger at that point with Dean Martin (Levy 205).

Sketch of the Pompadour Bedroom in Hollywood or Bust.
Courtesy of Henry Bumstead.

What I wish to focus on in the next two sketches from *Hollywood or Bust* is the amount of detail revealed in each sketch. Take the bedroom of a Las Vegas hotel, for instance. Let us immediately acknowledge the sheer mastery of the drawing itself. As many who have looked at such sketches have remarked, "I would like to frame that and put it on my wall." There is a very real artistic beauty in these sketches that goes far beyond mere functionalism of "what kind of set to design." No one thinks the film is great or even "pretty good." But the art work, beginning with the sketches, is first-rate. And, of course, nobody but the production team would ever see these.

The cliché among screenwriters is that "nobody ever paid to see a screenplay." The same is true of sketches for the sets, which mean so much to every film (be they constructed or found on location and adapted). Production designer Ken Adams, whose credits include *Around the World in 80 Days, Dr. No, You Only Live Twice, Dr. Strangelove, The Spy Who Loved Me,* and many others, puts it well when he emphasizes the importance of this phase—sketching—of the process: "I think it is advisable for anyone who wants to be a production designer to be able to freehand sketch" (LoBrutto 46). Bumstead couldn't agree more.

Consider more closely what each sketch reveals. Not only do we get a clear idea of what a set should look like, down to minute detail, but we also understand the "mood," tone, emotion, and thus what I would call the

The completed Pompadour Bedroom in Hollywood or Bust.
Courtesy of Henry Bumstead.

"inner spirit" of the scene. This interior Las Vegas casino sketch does not convey farce, slapstick, or even comedy at all. Once more, the emphasis is realism. It is a world of shadows, intrigue, glamour—with no one center for the eye to follow.

But Bumstead's sketches, as we will see throughout this study, reveal more than an artist's hand and an understanding of the essence of a particular screenplay in terms of theme, character, and plot. Equally important is what Ken Adams states (and Bumstead wholeheartedly agrees) is "an architectural understanding of space" (ibid.).

Now compare the shot of the actual set constructed from the sketch! Bumstead is surprised at my surprise at how close the final product is to the conception as sketched. For that is just how production design should work. But once more, as a viewer of thousands of films that I have enjoyed over the years without thinking about the sets and the design of the "look,"

I am still so impressed with the sheer professionalism of turning sketch into set.

Western Landscapes, Interior and External: *The Furies*

The Furies (1950); *directed by Anthony Mann; produced by Hal Wallis; written by Charles Schnee from the novel by Niven Busch; cinematography by Victor Milner. Cast: Barbara Stanwyck, Walter Huston, Wendell Corey, Gilbert Roland, Judith Anderson.*

Bummy has always enjoyed working on westerns. Certainly, as we will explore, his work with Clint Eastwood has become a lasting testimony to his skill in this most American of genres. But Bumstead's years at Paramount gave him a lot of experience, for he helped shape a stream of westerns, including *Streets of Laredo, The Redhead and the Cowboy, The Hangman, Run for Cover, Whispering Smith* (second unit work only), and *Union Pacific* (draftsman only).

Before taking a closer look at an early Bumstead western, let us ask the question that is not as simple as it seems: what is a western landscape, as seen in movies since the early days of cinema? Lee Clark Mitchell in *Westerns: Making the Man in Fiction and Film* has well described how connected the cinematic western landscape is tied to the idealized landscapes of western painters such as Charles Russell and authors such as James Fenimore Cooper. According to Mitchell, in both film and fiction the landscape photographed or described was "lending an illusion of realism to otherwise outrageous plots" (35).

The Furies is a psychological western with warring tension between a wealthy cattle rancher, C. T. Jeffords (Walter Huston in his final film role) and his daughter, Vance Jeffords (Stanwyck). Anthony Mann made a string of memorable westerns that deal with internal psychological warfare more than with the standard shoot-out of Wild West action stories: *Winchester 73* (1950), *Bend of the River* (1952), *The Man from Laramie* (1955), *The Far Country* (1954), and *The Last Frontier* (1956), to name but a few. Instead of John Wayne–like figures, most of Mann's western protagonists are wracked with self-doubt and Oedipal fears. As David Thomson notes, "Mann discovered his own Western sensibility which was to see human stories as small, and even aberrant, in the vastness of terrain" (477).

In such a vein, *The Furies* centers on a woman—Barbara Stanwyck— rather than a western male, and the plot of family intrigue between father

Sketch for the Jeffords ranch in The Furies.
Illustrator Ken Reid. Courtesy of Henry Bumstead.

and daughter, including a "shoot-out" scene between them and their followers, is closer to Greek tragedy than to *Gunfight at the OK Corral.* Because this is a "psychological Western," the emphasis is on interior shots rather than the kind of John Ford, Monument Valley exterior shots one usually thinks of when thinking "western."

At least half of the 109 minutes of the film take place inside the Jeffordses' ranch home: downstairs, on the grand staircase, upstairs, and on the front porch. The other interior sets include a saloon in town, several banks, a San Francisco hotel (interior and exterior), and an old hillside stone building used in the family shoot-out between the forces of father and daughter. Exteriors are more suggestive of evening than daytime, and while there are a few broad daylight vistas of the vast expanse of western territory, many of the exterior scenes are in tree-lined creekbeds at night or twilight hillsides, as in the final shot of Stanwyck and her newly acquired

Barbara Stanwyck and Wendell Corey in The Furies. *Courtesy of Henry Bumstead.*

husband riding off into the landscape, speaking of the grandchildren they hope to raise on their ranch, aptly named "The Furies."

The Jeffordses' Ranch

The Jeffordses' ranch is one of the most elaborate ranch sets I can remember seeing. In fact, the kind of grand scale of the rooms, suggesting both size and wealth, appear closer to southern mansions than to ranch

Hal Wallis (left) and Henry Bumstead working on The Furies.
Courtesy of Henry Bumstead.

houses on the lone prairie. The overall scheme that Bumstead settled on from his research was to work with a whitewashed adobe brick and dark woodwork.

In every sense, the ranch radiates "wealth." The grand staircase is twice as wide as anything else we remember from westerns, and the living room with its huge fireplace and large furniture also suggests that Jeffords has arrived and is not a "cowpoke" in the unschooled sense.

Because more than half the film takes place on this set, we feel we know it well, upstairs and downstairs, by the end of the film. And each room has its own personality. Thus, when the crucial scene of violence occurs— as Stanwyck throws scissors into the face of her father's new love, who is taking the place of her mother—the action occurs in her mother's upstairs lounge, the most "refined" and ornate room of the house. Bumstead has commented that he liked to work with the adobe look and the contrast between the white walls and dark wood. We might add too that this scheme is particularly effective for a strong black and white film.

The Saloon

Bumstead remarks that he worked with a standard "western street" at RKO for the brief street shots in *The Furies*, but all interiors, including the saloon, are his construction on the lot. In this case the saloon is also much more "layered" than typical western saloons that appear to be one long, large room with a long bar and a few scattered poker tables. Bummy's saloon has several rooms separated by walls with glass doors with names on them that get reflected off characters as they stand in the light.

The Hillside Hut

There is a big shoot-out between Stanwyck, working with some of the Mexican hands, and her father and his henchmen. Stanwyck and her supporters are in a crude stone house up on a hill as gunfire rages all around them. Bumstead says this simple house was constructed on location in Arizona. The interior shots of the house, however, were, once more, studio set. I can't remember seeing many crude stone houses in westerns; thus the texture Bummy has brought to the project adds a depth beyond that of the script and the acting.

San Francisco

The San Francisco sequence isn't long, but it involves interiors of a San Francisco hotel and exteriors, including one bank scene as Stanwyck tracks down her father's bankers in an effort to win the day, not on the battlefield of gunplay but by "out-banking" him. These sets are quite detailed and speak, once more, of a highly professional level of work under the pressure of time and limited budgeting.

Exterior Landscape Setups

Most western landscapes are shot in Arizona, and they do give us that special feeling of space and magnitude that westerns can convey. Because of the psychological nature of this tale, however, Bumstead helped choose locations that included tree-shaded, dry riverbeds shot at evening or night rather than the standard wide-horizon daylight shots of so many westerns, including John Ford's films. Thus, while there was no need for Bumstead to build sets for such shots, the orchestration of light and shadow and working closely with the cinematographer became very important.

In another western that Bumstead worked on, *Run for Cover*, he displayed his finely tuned sense of a western town in its environment. We have all seen the very simple standard western street town in so many films, with a saloon and sheriff's office, a blacksmith's shop, and a general store. But Bumstead's vision produces a much wider street, buildings spaced farther apart, and a strong sense of mountains and a world outside the town (the actual street was a location in Silverton, Colorado, with some construction on location and some at the studio's back lot).

Production Design and War: *The Bridges at Toko-Ri*
The Bridges at Toko-Ri (1954); *directed by Mark Robson; produced by Perlberg-Seaton; written by Valentine Davies from the novel by James Michener; cinematography by Loyal Griggs. Cast: Grace Kelly, Fredric March, Mickey Rooney, Earl Holliman, Robert Strauss.*

The Bridges at Toko-Ri, an action thriller shot in 1953 and released the following year, is based on James Michener's novel about the futility of the Korean War and the conflict and drama among American navy pilots.

The film won an Oscar for the special effects, made from filming the one-third scale miniature of the bombing of the bridges. But clearly Bumstead's work of dealing with all the carrier interiors, filmed on stages, planes, and battlefields, paid off to make this one of the most memorable of the "futility of war" films produced by Hollywood.

Almost 100 percent of *My Friend Irma* was a studio film; *The Furies* demanded perhaps 20 percent of on-location shooting in Arizona, but about 40 percent of *The Bridges at Toko-Ri* was shot on location in the Tokyo Bay area and in the San Fernando Valley, which was the location for the ending trench war shots as well as the construction of the miniature bridges. Bummy says they spent a month at sea and in and around Tokyo shooting street scenes. Many of the carrier landings were actually dangerous, as they shot on the aircraft carrier USS *Oriskany*. As Bumstead remembers, they lost a camera when it was hit by a plane.

I've included some of Bummy's rough sketches for the storyboard to suggest how well he helped conceive the look of the aerial action, which depended on constant cutting between studio closeups in cockpits, on ship decks, and such, spliced to actual on-location aerial shots. Thus, while "special effects" is a separate Oscar from production design, the responsibility for storyboarding and setting up "the look" fell to Bumstead.

Of course, the action of the flying is memorable. But most of the screen time is taken up, as is often true in action thrillers too, with ship interiors of the bridge, briefing room, crew's quarters, captain's quarters, and so forth. These sets are impressive because they do not call attention to themselves. If the ranch in *The Furies* announces "wealth," the navy "on board" sets for *The Bridges at Toko-Ri* are dull grays and soft greens and low ceilings of the captain's quarters as he discusses William Holden's interrupted life as a civilian to become a navy pilot. To actually study these sets is to see how much work went into the details of a room's overhead pipes, bland towels, and various knobs on the wall. In terms of sets, perhaps the most impressive turns out to be a dance held with a band in a rotating shaft and the ship decked out to look like a nightclub. This was the only interior filmed in Tokyo.

The Tokyo hotel in the film was all done on the stage: the lobby, dining rooms, communal baths, and more, which Bumstead is rightly proud of. But the scene in which Holden and Mickey Rooney die in the ditch was shot in the San Fernando Valley.

Clever use of split screen was also part of Bumstead's bag of tricks for *The Bridges*. In the shot of the aircraft carriers, the right-hand side of the frame is actually a split screen. The aircraft carrier on the left was flipped over to give the effect of two aircraft carriers, side by side. But in actuality there was only one ship on the left and a hill and a dock on the right. Director Mark Robeson was upset when he saw the hill there, but Bumstead showed him how they could do the "flip" of the real ship to create two!

The Art of Low-Budget Horror:
I Married a Monster from Outer Space
I Married a Monster from Outer Space (1958), *directed and produced by Gene Fowler Jr.; written by Louis Vittes; cinematography by Haskell Boggs. Cast: Tom Tryon, Gloria Talbott, Ken Lynch, John Eldridge. A revamping of Don Siegel's* Invasion of the Body Snatchers, *made just two years earlier.*

This low-budget, swiftly made sci-fi horror tale has become a cult film over the years. Of course, Bumstead had no idea what future this film

317 S.P.D. MINIATURE - BRUBAKERS POINT OF VIEW -
MOVING SHOT. DIVE AND PULL OUT - 2ND BRIDGE
BLOWING UP - SMOKE CLEARING ON 1ST BRIDGE.

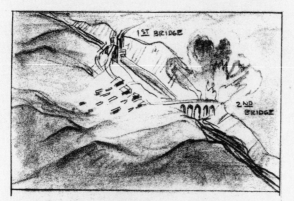

318 S.P.D. MINIATURE BACKGROUND - MOVING
SIDE ANGLE - BOTTOM OF DIVE. GUN
FIRE ETC. PULL OUT.

322 (A) S.P.D. ROYS VIEW OF VALLEY
AND BRIDGES - No 2 BRIDGE
STILL STANDING.

327 - PROCESS- BRU BAKER WATCHES LEE.

328 S.P.D. MINIATURE - LEE'S PLANES GO THRU AND DROP BOMBS ON I T BRIDGE.

Sketches for the bridge-bombing sequence in The Bridges at Toko-Ri.
Courtesy of Henry Bumstead.

would have, and in fact he does not remember being influenced by the earlier and more popular tale, *Invasion of the Body Snatchers,* which shares much of the same premise of aliens entering human bodies and becoming something like living zombies.

The challenge in both cases, however, was to create a sense of the eerie without much of a budget and thus without high-tech special effects and sets. Ironically, the comments of film historian David Thomson on *Invasion* apply equally to Bumstead's work on *I Married a Monster*—that it is an "exemplary science fiction because it needs no visual tricks and knows that zombies and vital people look alike" (694).

Bumstead laughs when he thinks about this project, not only because of the extremely tiny budget he had to deal with, but also because of an incident that occurred in recent years when he visited Australia. He had been on a radio talk show and soon after was met by a woman who came running up, saying, "Mr. Bumstead, you worked on my favorite film of all

Matte and split-screen scene in The Bridges at Toko-Ri. *Courtesy of Henry Bumstead.*

time!" Of course he was expecting to hear something like *Vertigo, To Kill a Mockingbird,* or *Slaughterhouse-Five,* but instead the woman beamed and said, *"I Married a Monster from Outer Space!"*

One has to remember that many sci-fi films of the period actually had lavish budgets for sets. The MGM film *Forbidden Planet* (1956), taking a futuristic spin on Shakespeare's *The Tempest,* had very elaborate sets designed by the great MGM production designer Cedric Gibbons, whose name appeared on more movies than any other production designer (Stephens 113).

For starters, money was saved on *I Married a Monster* because more than half the film is set at night and much of it on a stage set, so there really isn't much to see! And unlike *Forbidden Planet,* which had to show us another planet, *I Married a Monster* is sci-fi that grows out of the ordinary and, once more, reality as we know it.

The plot is centered on a young couple who are engaged to be married. Just before the wedding, the groom, Bill (Tom Tryon), is taken over by the aliens, so he is an alien zombie. We learn later that all the women died on the aliens' planet; thus this "body snatching" campaign is a survival-of-the-species program. The sets consist of the young couple's home, a local

Local citizens approaching the monsters' spaceship in I Married a Monster from Outer Space. *Copyright © 1958 by Paramount Pictures Corporation.*

bar, a doctor's office, a police office, a justice of the peace office, and a suburban street.

Monsters and the space theme? Cinema has combined the two motifs since the silent days of Murnau's *Nosferatu* (1922). We see the aliens only three or four times, and briefly at that. And they are accompanied by a black cloud of smoke and fuzzy electronic noise. The alien spacecraft appears only as a dark frame with an angular gate being lowered and a bright light inside. We also briefly see the radarlike antennae of the spacecraft, looking more like enlarged food-processing blenders than anything as functional as alien surveillance gear.

Finally, the interior of the spacecraft is vintage plywood in looks, with an actual ladder on one side next to the human males hanging by their necks from the ceiling. That's it! Several critics have caught on to the fact that besides being campy, the film is actually something of a feminist statement (Halliwell 529). Much of the film is told from the point of view of the young wife (Gloria Talbott) who is trying to deal with why her husband acts, well, just so *strangely*! Thus she has some of the best lines, such as asking her alien husband at one point, "Does frightening women make you proud?"

Bumstead has underlined this theme with the warmly domestic home where much of the film takes place. It is the wife's touch that we assume accounts for the bright paintings and the cabinet full of books, for instance. The production design therefore supports the loving touch that the bride wants to see in her marriage since the alien has no clue as to emotions or culture.

Yes, there is a happy ending. The real husband returns as the aliens leave, and we can only hope that this couple will become a loving one in the pleasant suburban California home that Bumstead constructed with no budget. They may even read all of the books in the book cabinet as the years go by, something that aliens definitely would never do!

two

The Hitchcock Films
"Never in My Wildest Dreams!"

Hitch was a master at combining sets with location shots.
HENRY BUMSTEAD

"Never in my wildest dreams," Bumstead remarks, "did I ever believe I would work with Alfred Hitchcock!" After all these years, there is still a wide smile on his face when he explains what an unexpected opportunity it was.

It was 1956, and he was working on *The Vagabond King*, a rendition of the often-told story of the French poet François Villon and a remake of the Ronald Colman film *If I Were King* (1938), scripted by Preston Sturges. Michael Curtiz was the director, and Bummy's challenge was to create a Gothic look on the Paramount lot. "I mean to tell you, Gothic separates the men from the boys," says Bummy. "During my early years as an apprentice at Paramount I did a lot of Gothic detail. Gothic is a tough style, but I learned a lot from Hans Dreier about how to do Gothic well." The Hitchcock contact came through Robert Burks, who was the cinematographer on *Vagabond King* and also Hitchcock's cameraman.[1] At that time Hitchcock asked Burks if he knew any young art directors that he would like to work with, and he said he was working with one—Henry Bumstead. "'Have him come up and see me,' Hitch said. And that's how I got the job," comments Bumstead. "How lucky can you be!" And that led to four films with Hitchcock: *The Man Who Knew Too Much* (1956), *Vertigo* (1958), *Topaz* (1969), and *Family Plot* (1976).

*Bumstead (left) with Hitchcock (center) and Howard Kazanjian,
the assistant director of* Family Plot. *Courtesy of Henry Bumstead.*

What is immediately fascinating about this collaboration is that Hitchcock began his career as an art/production designer from 1922 to 1925, working with director Graham Cutts (Spoto 4). The point that everyone has made about Hitch, therefore, that he "edited in his head" and knew every shot of a film before he began shooting is surely a product of those early "art directing" years when he would storyboard films for production.

In fact, Hitch continued to provide his production designers with his own very rough sketches to give them an idea of what he had in mind. Bumstead's set for Scottie's apartment in *Vertigo* is based on Hitch's original sketch.

Need we say more? Actually, we should, and I am referring to Bumstead's ability as one of the finest of Hollywood's production designers to bring out the inner spirit and "soul" of a project, a film, a director's vision. In this case, Bumstead learned to illustrate, amplify, and articulate Hitchcock's predominant themes, which sound perhaps rather abstract when listed but which are clearly within each film that Hitch made. These themes are, according to *Christian Science Monitor* film critic David Sterritt, the ambiguity of guilt and innocence, the transference of guilt and innocence from one individual to another, the fascination with a guilty

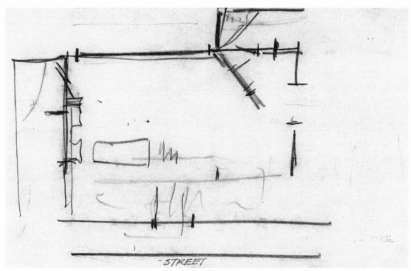

Hitchcock's drawing of Scottie's room in Vertigo. *Courtesy of Henry Bumstead.*

Bumstead's final design for Scottie's room in Vertigo. *Courtesy of Henry Bumstead.*

woman, the therapeutic function of obsession and vulnerability, and the equation of danger and knowledge (7). Bumstead does not express his understanding of the four Hitchcock films he worked on this way. But in designing for and with Hitch he was able to intuit these moods and emotional states that the master of suspense was after.

Hitch has always been held up as a prime example of an "auteur"—a director who shaped his own vision with each film, making it absolutely "a film by Alfred Hitchcock." And of course he encouraged this stardom of the director outlook in many ways, as he himself appeared in his films and exercised tight control over every aspect of the film.

But everyone who worked with him understood that Hitch was Hitch in large part because he assembled wonderful teams of professionals to work with him. Many of his films were shot by Robert Burks, for instance, and another production designer who worked frequently with Hitch was Robert Boyle (*Sabateur, North by Northwest, The Birds,* and *Marnie*). Boyle highlighted this collaborative point when he noted, "Hitchcock availed himself of the best help he could get. . . . He would even listen to his chauffeur, he was so secure in his own abilities" (LoBrutto 12). Thus "auteur" did not mean the work of Hitchcock alone, but of Hitchcock's ability to have a vision and assemble a wonderful team.

"TRY USING MIRRORS, BUMMY!": DESIGNING HITCHCOCK

How was working with Hitchcock?

Bumstead: I had a very good relationship with Hitch. He was always very nice to me. For instance, Hitch had prostate trouble, and when he found out I had had it too, I got a call right away, "Come down to Hitchcock's office!" So we would discuss prostate problems, since I had recently had an operation then. I would always go down to show him drawings, and he would be reading the *London Times*. So maybe on any given day I would have six or seven drawings of sets to show him, and I would get through showing him about two of them when Hitch would begin to yawn. "Bummy, carry on along those lines, you're doing fine!" And he would start reading the paper again.

Whenever I had a problem and I was really trying to get Hitch to comment, he would always say something like, "Try using mirrors, Bummy!" I learned a lot from Hitch. He knew how to make the sets look like the characters he was filming, and Hans Dreier was the same. So the stamp collection in *Vertigo* was an important character detail [for Jimmy Stewart]. I placed stamp magazines and such on the set. Hitch liked those kinds of details. Or I would have a musical instrument if the character played an instrument.

Once you knew you would be working for Hitchcock, did you "study" his films before you actually went to work?

Bummy (left) looking over plans for Vertigo *with Hitchcock, production manager C. O. "Doc" Erickson (second from left), and associate producer Herbert Coleman (right). Courtesy of Henry Bumstead.*

Bumstead: No, I never studied Hitch's films, but I had seen many of them. For instance, I hadn't seen Hitch's original *The Man Who Knew Too Much* (1934) before I started working on his remake version. Remember that Hitch had once been an art director himself. So one thing I really admired about him was that whatever you built, he really shot. He didn't just get in a corner and shoot. He used sets well. He shot every bit of your set. And I worked well with Bob Burks, his cameraman.

It is always said that Hitchcock had planned his film so well that he knew every shot and therefore could be very economical about his shooting and thus his editing. Did you find this to be true?

Bumstead: Hitch *did* know every shot. And he was impatient about how long it took to light a set. One day he was waiting for the lighting to be set up, and he was sitting there pouting, as usual, with that look he always had on his face, and I asked him what he was thinking about. And Hitch said, "I'm thinking about my next film. Waiting around here is terribly *boring.*" Hitch always said, "The cameraman has more time on the set than I have with the actors." It was amazing to watch him because he would shoot part of a scene, yell "cut," and then tell the cameraman, "Now a 40mm on this person." He knew each shot and lens exactly. George Tomasceni was his editor, but because of the way the film was shot, it was already cut, really. I know that Hitch never went to watch dailies. He just went to the finished film. He only went if he was told there were problems.

Was there a particular Hitchcock "rhythm" to shooting a film?

Bumstead: They always figured Hitch for two and a half pages a day. That would mean about seventy days of shooting.

You had worked with so many directors before you worked with Hitch. Besides the remarks you have already made, how was Hitch different?

Bumstead: I liked it that Hitch didn't start shooting until about nine-thirty, so you could get a lot of work done before the shooting began. And he hardly ever filmed after five P.M. I liked that! The only bad thing working with Hitch was that somehow everyone seemed to have Hitch's production account number, so a lot of things got charged to Hitch that had nothing to do with his films. That was terrible. It was very different from working with Hal Wallis. With Hal you had to have the set done to the penny you agreed upon or it was hell.

You say he would sometimes have you up to his second home in Santa Cruz, California, like he did when you were filming Vertigo. *What was a weekend at the Hitchcocks' like?*

Bumstead: Very British! I went up to Santa Cruz for his birthday when we were making *Vertigo,* for instance. His daughter Pat was there, and we were on the veranda as the phone was ringing with well-wishers. Hitch was quite a guy. I couldn't keep up with him. You know, he would even carry your bags up to your room. He had terrific energy. I couldn't drink as much as he could, either. I would have to go to bed by midnight, and even then I would be dead the next morning. But not Hitch. Early the next day, his complexion (pink!) would look like a baby's butt that had just been spanked!

The Man Who Knew Too Much

The Man Who Knew Too Much (1956); directed and produced by
Alfred Hitchcock for Paramount Pictures; written by John Michael Hayes
from the story by Charles Bennett and D. B. Wyndham Lewis; cinema-
tography by Robert Burks. Cast: James Stewart, Doris Day, Bernard Miles,
Brenda De Banzie, Christopher Olsen, Reggie Nalder, Daniel Gelin,
and Ralph Truman.

The Man Who Knew Too Much is one of those rare cases when a filmmaker remakes his own work. Hitchcock's original version was shot in 1934 and set in St. Moritz and London as a family on holiday in the Alps witness the murder of a close friend and have their own daughter kidnapped. As Stuart McDougal notes, "The film is a study of the dynamics of a marriage as well as the conditions of spectatorship and passivity (related to both marriage and film viewing)" (54).

The film builds as the husband, Bob (Leslie Banks), and his sharp-shooting wife, Jill (Edna Best), track down an international conspiracy in a showdown in the Royal Albert Hall during a concert. Hitchcock himself made it clear that he was never satisfied with the way this earlier version worked out its conclusion (McDougal 55), thus the attempt to set things right in the remake. The result is a film that is highly entertaining but one that many critics, including Robin Wood, feel "has been seriously under-estimated" (359).

What changes is characterization and location, as we now have an American family—the husband, Dr. Ben McKenna, is played by James Stewart and his wife, Jo Conway McKenna, once a professional singer, is performed by Doris Day. And instead of the Alps we now have an overcrowded Marrakech in North Africa and what seems like a rather deserted London. In terms of character development, more than a plot-driven story, as in the original tale, Hitchcock now focuses on the emerging identity of Jo Conway as she comes to reconcile motherhood with her past career as a well-known singer. In fact, it is her singing of "Que Sera, Sera" that becomes key to the reworked conclusion of the film, played out in the Royal Albert Hall in what has been described as "one of the great set pieces in Hitchcock's work" (McDougal 64).

The challenge for Henry Bumstead was to capture both worlds—North Africa and London—as the strongly contrasting realities they suggest for the story that Hitch wanted to, at last, "set straight." He succeeded well

Sketch for the McKennas' hotel room in Morocco in The Man Who Knew Too Much. *Courtesy of Henry Bumstead.*

with such a complex task, with sets ranging from the interiors of the hotel in Marrakech to the excellent reproductions of portraits from the Royal Albert Hall. Hitch was to use Bummy for three more films.

Were there a lot of sets to build for The Man Who Knew Too Much?
Bumstead: On *The Man Who Knew Too Much*, you have to remember that other than the exterior scenes, almost everything else was a set. A young art director looking at *Vertigo* would think Hitch shot in actual rooms, but that's not true—they're all sets! I remember when I was in North Africa doing pre-production on *The Man Who Knew Too Much*. I bought a lot of things, such as cloth and tile and lamps and other objects, because I knew I had to build all the interiors. I took lots of photos, for instance, of the wonderful tile work over there. We shot in an old hotel in Marrakech, La Mamounia, which was closed at the time. So I took pictures and did research and made backings there. I think all these things pleased Hitch. He always felt he could get a better performance from his actors on a set. For this reason, when you worked with Hitch, you got stage space if you needed it, and we did need lots.

But Hitch often combined sets with location shots. Hitch always had two or three things he was very adamant about that he told you he wanted to do in the picture. One point in *The Man Who Knew Too Much* was the back of the church in London when they leave: part was

Sketch for the Moroccan restaurant in The Man Who Knew Too Much.
Courtesy of Henry Bumstead.

location, part matte, part a set. All three combined gave the effect he
wanted.

How much time before a shoot would you be on location for Hitch?

Bumstead: That depends, but we were always several weeks ahead of the
shoot to get things ready and do some building. And I had to choose
locations. Luckily Hitch liked almost every location I ever chose on
his films. But Marrakech was terribly hot. We were there three weeks
shooting exteriors. The dye marketplace where cloth was strung on overhead poles was the scene where a hand grenade was really thrown by
Arabs. That scared Hitch enough for him to start directing shots from
the front seat of a car. All of this danger was a reaction of the native
Arabs against the French, who controlled Marrakech at the time. Before we finished filming in Africa, I moved on to England to get locations and sets ready for filming—these included the church, the U.S.
embassy, and the Royal Albert Hall, too. To find the church in London,
I rode around for two days. Someone said the one we finally used was
the same one that appears in the British version of *The Man Who Knew
Too Much*. But I don't know, I never looked to see.[2]

Some important shots were made in Albert Hall, but we built sets for much of it, too. This was especially true for the upper-level boxes of the hall, and also the rooms of the embassy, including the stairs where the boy hears Doris Day singing. These were all sets. And to prepare such sets, I took pictures of everything. Even hardware in stores! That's the marvelous thing about my job: research. We built sets in England we didn't get to use because Hitch was lonely and wanted to get home. He missed Alma, his wife. So he wanted me to return home early and get the sets ready for filming. Thus, four or five more sets in England were never used.

Besides your assigned work, was there a pleasure in working on this film?
Bumstead: I liked Doris Day a lot. I remember in Marrakech sitting on the floor of a restaurant eating couscous with Doris. Jimmy Stewart was wonderful, too. He was like an old shoe! One day before we started filming, I walked into Hitch's office, and he played me a song on tape. It was "Que Sera, Sera." And he asked me what I thought. I thought it was wonderful, and Hitch looked pleased!

Vertigo

Vertigo (1958); *directed and produced by Alfred Hitchcock for Paramount Pictures; written by Alec Coppel and Samuel Taylor from the novel* D'entre les morts *by Pierre Boileau; cinematography by Robert Burks. Cast: James Stewart, Kim Novak, Barbara Bel Geddes, Tom Helmore, Konstantin Shayne, Henry Jones, Raymond Bailey, and Ellen Corby.*

Vertigo remains as one of Hitchcock's best-remembered films, especially in the restored print that was meticulously assembled by Robert A. Harris and James C. Katz and released in 1996. The excellent documentary that accompanies the video and DVD version of that release, *Obsessed with Vertigo*, follows the path of the restoration and includes interviews with many associated with the film, including Henry Bumstead. Martin Scorsese is also interviewed and sets the tone and theme of the whole film in saying, "I was drawn into *Vertigo* like being drawn into an obsession." Many viewers would echo similar comments, including Donald Spoto in his study of Hitchcock. Spoto notes that he was in prep school when he first saw *Vertigo* and was so overwhelmed and disturbed "by the impact of its images that it altered my perception of life, of art and myself. The twenty-six times I have seen the film since have deepened those reactions" (291).

Hitchcock's daughter, Pat, called this strong visual nature found in *Vertigo* "pure cinema" (Spoto 292), and she accurately identifies the power of the camera work and the set design by Henry Bumstead, which perfectly captures the emotions and themes of the story. For few films have dealt so thoroughly with human obsession and the conflicting worlds of attraction and repulsion as seen in the obsession of detective Scottie (James Stewart) with Judy/Madeleine (Kim Novak), reaching across the complicated plot involving "death" and Scottie's fear of heights.

Bumstead had been working in the Hollywood studio system for twenty-one years when he signed on for this memorable project. And this first Oscar nomination for him was more than well deserved, as any re-viewing of the film will demonstrate.

I understand that Vertigo *did not start off as a smooth production.*

Bumstead: There were a lot of problems at first. When we got on *Vertigo*, Hitch wanted Vera Miles, but she was pregnant; then he settled on Kim Novak. Meanwhile he had spent quite a lot of time in San Francisco looking for locations. Hitch didn't know what kind of businessman to make the husband who contacts Jimmy Stewart, but after scouting with Herbie Coleman and Doc Erickson, we made him a shipbuilder. So we made the background plates of the shipbuilding and cranes in the background.

By the way, Hitch liked the set I did for the shipbuilder's office so much that he had me come out to his house after the finish of *Vertigo* and work on one of his rooms! It's funny. One morning I was going to work and I saw Alma before going to my office and she said, "Did Hitch ever tell you how much he loves the room you did?" I said, "No!" And when I got into my office, I was told to go immediately to Hitch's office. He wanted to tell me how much he liked the room. For his other house in Santa Cruz, in the mountains, I designed some outdoor furniture and some iron gates and grilles.

How was working on Vertigo *different from, say,* The Man Who Knew Too Much?

Bumstead: Well, the opening scene was so important in *Vertigo*. We filmed several places in Los Angeles from ten stories high, which was the limit for buildings in those days because of earthquakes. But they gave us no feeling of height. So finally we did a "forced perspective," which made it seem about fifty stories high, and Hitch was very pleased with that.[3]

3A-Scottie Tries to Recover-Slides Backwards
Set Plus Transp.

5-Scottie's Viewpoint - Gap Trebles its Depth S.P.D.

3B-Scottie Swings into Space -Set plus Transp.

6-Nausea Overcomes Scottie - Set plus Transp.

4-Scottie Looks Down - Set plus Transp.

7-Policeman Returns-Fleeing Criminal in the
Distance - Set plus Transp.

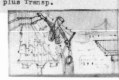

Storyboard for the opening scene of Vertigo. *Courtesy of Henry Bumstead.*

8-Policeman Strains to Reach Down to
Scottie - Set plus Transp.

12-Scottie Hears Wild Cry - Set plus Transp.
Policeman falls through shot Behind Scottie

9-Scottie's Viewpoint - The Alley Below - S.P.D.

13-Policeman Falling Thru Space - S.P.D.

10-Policeman Endeavors to Stretch Out His
Hand Further - Set plus Sky Backing

14-Scottie Stares Down in Horror - Set
Set plus Transp.

11-Tiles Give Way - Policeman Starts to Slide
Set plus Transp.

15-Policeman Sprawled on Ground - People
Stare at Body and Look up to Scottie - S.P.D.

FROM THE DEAD – INT. TOWER & STAIRCASE

Storyboard for the bell tower scene in Vertigo. *Courtesy of Henry Bumstead.*

Of course, I enjoyed designing the church tower and steps leading up to the bell tower. You know you could never get Hitch to go and look at a set, and the bell tower was completed. So I asked Herbie Coleman [the associate producer] to bring Hitch over. Herbie asked Hitch to come over, and Hitch said, "Isn't Bummy a professional? So why do I have to go look at it?"

Some mornings I was rather nervous because you would be waiting for Hitch to arrive and look at the set. All the driving scenes, for instance, we did in the studio with rear projection. You know how most directors now hate rear projection and want to be in a real car hanging on to the sides! But Bob Burks was such a good cinematographer that he really knew how to make those plates for the process shots. I always work carefully with a cameraman, the set dresser, and with the costume designer, Edith Head. I did about thirty films with her.

How did Vertigo *do at the box office?*

Bumstead: I really don't know. But its reputation grew. *Psycho* and *Rear*

FROM THE DEAD - INT. TOWER & STAIRCASE

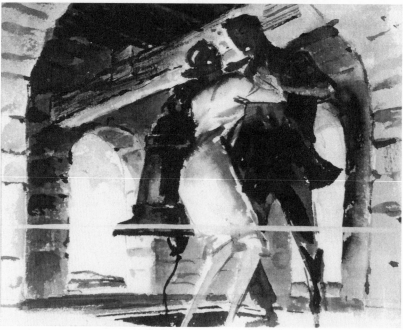

Sketch of the mission in Vertigo. *Courtesy of Henry Bumstead.*

Storyboard of the bridge scene in Vertigo. *Courtesy of Henry Bumstead.*

Still of the bridge scene in Vertigo. *Copyright © 1983 by Universal City Studios, Inc. Courtesy of Henry Bumstead.*

Window were probably the most popular during Hitch's lifetime. You know, it's a shame, but Hitch never got an Oscar for any of his films. He wasn't very social in Hollywood and didn't campaign for awards. He had a small circle of friends such as Grace Kelly, Cary Grant, and Jimmy Stewart. But he didn't go to Hollywood parties like the rest of the directors did. It was too bad. But what a great body of work he did through the years.

Topaz

Topaz (1969); *directed and produced by Alfred Hitchcock for Universal Pictures; written by Samuel Taylor from the novel by Leon Uris; cinematography by John F. Warren. Cast: John Forsythe, Frederick Stafford, Dany Robin, Karin Dor, John Vernon, Michel Piccoli, Philippe Noiret, and Claude Jade.*

Critic Robin Wood has summed up the feeling of many about *Topaz:* "It must surely be one of the most uneven films in the history of cinema in which something approaching Hitchcock's best rubs shoulders with his very worst" (222). In contrast to projects like *The Man Who Knew*

Watercolor rendition of Hotel Theresa in Topaz. *Courtesy of Henry Bumstead.*

Too Much and *Vertigo,* in which Hitchcock had a strong personal interest from the beginning, *Topaz* was a novel acquired by Universal and basically assigned to Hitchcock. Thus from the start we have a blockbuster book with far too complicated a plot and too much material and too many locations for any one film. It was a bad bargain all around from the beginning.

And yet, as always, Bumstead was a pro and carried off very complicated sets and locations as well as he could. These comments were made by Bumstead while we watched the film on video once more together. He also claims it was the most rushed film he ever worked on.

Topaz *was not one of Hitchcock's most successful films.*
Bumstead: You know, it is actually a very difficult picture to follow. I was working on *Airport* with director George Seaton at the time. But I was called off to work with Hitch on *Topaz.* The problem was, Hitch never had a completed script, just an outline treatment, and off he went to scout locations and start shooting in Copenhagen. We went to New York, where Hitch always stayed at the St. Regis, so no surprise that we used it in the film. We scouted Harlem and found the Theresa Hotel mentioned in the book, but it was an insurance company at that time. So I had to make it back into a hotel on the back lot at Universal! I did

find lots of photos that helped me build the interior of it. Then we went to Copenhagen and started filming. Hitch was also casting as we went along. Then from Copenhagen to Germany and then to Paris. Luckily I had worked in Paris, so I knew people to contact for help.

It was a tough film! We left Paris and went to Washington, D.C., then to New York and home to California. My first day home I got word Hitch wanted to start filming in two weeks. I had to get three assistants and four decorators to get so many sets done. All those European locations and sets demanded a lot of ornament and detail. But I did get it all going, and I did a beautiful set for the exterior and interior of the Theresa Hotel. In fact, I did the whole block, including a Chock Full O' Nuts building and the interior of the hotel. Hitch said it looked so good that everyone would think we actually filmed those scenes in New York.

Can you describe some of the sets you enjoyed making for Topaz?

Bumstead (watching scenes in the film): See the flower shops and everything in this New York sequence? We built all of that on the back lot and a matte shot. It was a lot of rushed work. The interior of the flower shop of course is a set. Now you see the actors go inside the shop, and we can't hear them. Hitch did a lot of that: he liked scenes where we don't hear everything that is being said. Perhaps it was the influence of working in the silent period. Hitch said he would love to tell a whole story, a whole film, without dialogue!

There is a shot of the St. Regis Hotel in New York that you built as a set.

Bumstead (continuing to watch the video): Look at that hotel corridor. It was a forced perspective. Hitch loved it. No wonder I had high blood pressure! I got high blood pressure on *Topaz* and I'm still taking pills. However, I have it under control now. One of the toughest assignments I ever had, yes. When I look at *Topaz*, I can't believe I did it. It was a nightmare of work. But it came out well, thanks to the good help I had at the studio.

We see Castro's room in the hotel—there's a beer bottle in the foreground. Did you decide even that detail?

Bumstead: Yes, Castro drank beer, so we put that in. No, it wasn't in the script. [We now see an action scene in the New York streets.] All of this New York action sequence was on the back lot. I built all of this. It's a combination of back lot and matte shots. Now the next shot of the French ambassador's house is a real house in Georgetown. [We now see a scene of stock film from Cuba.] We did mix stock documentary film with the studio set.

With so many locations and such a difficult shoot, why do you think Hitch took on Topaz?

Bumstead: I don't know why. Casting was also hard, as I mentioned. John Forsythe was the only one they really wanted. On top of all that, the ending was tough. And yet there were some good sequences. Hitch had a script, *No Bail for the Judge,* and he wanted to make it with Audrey Hepburn and Laurence Harvey, so I spent one month in London researching the project with Hitch and Herbie Coleman. Audrey Hepburn was supposed to play a prostitute in order to catch the villain, and she wouldn't do it. So the picture was canceled, thank goodness.

Family Plot
Family Plot (1976); *directed and produced by Alfred Hitchcock; written by Ernest Lehman after the novel* The Rainbird Pattern *by Victor Canning; cinematography by Leonard South. Cast: Karen Black, Bruce Dern, Barbara Harris, William Devane, Ed Lauter, and Cathleen Nesbitt.*

Family Plot was Hitchcock's final film. And although Hitch did not think of it as his finale when he shot it, there is much that is "pure Hitchcock" in this tale of two very different couples who accidentally meet, one searching for the lost heir to a fortune and the other a couple of thieves (including the real heir).

With a working title of *Deceit* until near the end of production, "Family Plot" as a title also embraced a number of Hitchcock's themes over his fifty-seven films, including the influence of the dead over the living (Spoto 452), mistaken identities, and a long chase, in this case an elaborate car chase sequence.

Singled out for praise by many critics are the cemetery sequences, which do not quite rival *Vertigo*, comments Donald Spoto, but are "compelling nonetheless" (457). He goes on to credit Henry Bumstead for this powerful effect, stating that Bumstead found just the right cemetery in the Pioneer Cemetery in Sierra Madre, and the sequence was shot in two days of drizzle without artificial light. The effect is extraordinarily beautiful. "Some shots were made from a high point atop a thirty-foot scaffold" (ibid.).

As a "final take" on the importance of storyboarding for Hitch, one of the most important studies of his films, *The Art of Alfred Hitchcock,* by

Bummy (pointing) and Hitchcock on Family Plot. *Courtesy of Henry Bumstead.*

Donald Spoto, ends with thirty-five pages of the *Family Plot* storyboard but with no mention of Henry Bumstead in this section! Spoto's study is, of course, most useful for film scholars and cineasts in general. But the absence of discussion or mention of the art director/production designer who has made such a contribution to the final effect of the film is simply indicative of the need for more studies of figures such as Henry Bumstead who have shaped the way the films we admire look and affect us all.

What about Family Plot?

Bumstead: Hitch was getting older, about seventy-seven then, and *Family Plot* was his last film. But he did well, considering. For instance, Hitch had a bungalow at Universal, and he would drive up and in eight or ten steps he would be at his desk. Then at the end of a day's work, the limo would take him home, and six or eight steps—he was in his kitchen. Their house was by the Bel-Air golf course, and a slice ball could wind up in their yard. He had no grille covering the windows, so balls often came through his windows. But he kept glass to replace the broken windows, and as soon as one broke, he called the Bel-Air Country Club and they came right down and fixed it!

I picked all the locations on *Family Plot*. And I think the cemetery was one of the most important sets; I found it close by here in Los Angeles. I talked them into letting the weeds grow and everything in exchange for us fixing everything up afterward. I don't know how we were able to do that, but we did. We had marvelous weather. Lenny South, Bob Burks's camera operator for many years, was now cameraman [Burks passed away in 1968].

We shot in Los Angeles and in San Francisco. Hitch had a pacemaker by then. And whenever we went by plane, his pacemaker set off the alarms. Ollie was his driver in the San Francisco area. He was an ex-ambulance driver and Hitch loved him. We got a speeding ticket. Policemen scare Hitch, and it was so funny because the policeman wanted Hitch's autograph, but he was afraid to ask. We shot the chase scene in the mountains nearby. Someone asked Hitch how he found such places, and Hitch told him, "The only person who can find such places [is an] art director like Henry Bumstead."

We were shooting a big exterior shot one night in San Francisco and it was cold. We were all ready to shoot and Hitch drove up in his Lincoln limo and rolled down his window two or three inches, and I was almost knocked over by the brandy fumes and cigar smoke—he had obviously had a good dinner. And Hitch asked, "What are we doing here?" "Well, Hitch, we have lots of filming to do here." "But how do you expect me to get good performances in this cold?" I started to answer him but didn't. He said, "I think we better do this back in the studio." And I started to answer him when he said, "That's the trouble with you young art directors. You have no imagination." Well, I wasn't so young then, but there was no arguing with Hitch. Hitch then said, "When I was an art director back at UFA in Germany, I did a whole picture on one stage eighty feet by eighty feet." Of course I wanted to say—but didn't—"Well, Hitch, what kind of set was it, a bedroom?" So Hitch says we'll do it at the studio. And his window went up and he drove away.

This changed our shooting schedule. Then I had to scramble. A sloping street and alley and lots of construction. We did it all, and it was a beautiful set. We were ready to shoot, and Hitch drove onto the set. Yes, he drove onto the set! He got out, got into his director's chair. "Well, now, this is more like it!" he said. I was about to leave when he called to me and said, "Bummy, my friends in San Francisco tell me that of all the corners to shoot in the city, you chose the coldest!" And he asked, "How did you do that?" And I said, "Well, Hitch, it wasn't easy."

What's the bird?

Henry Bumstead '57

Bummy's caricature of Hitchcock. Courtesy of Henry Bumstead.

You know, Hitch always simplified things. On *Family Plot* an assistant came up and said, "We have four or five cars in this film, and we want to know what color the cars are." And Hitch replied, "I don't care what color the cars are as long as we know who is in each car!"

One story I do wish to add was when we were leaving San Francisco after a scouting trip. We get to the airport, and a stretch DC-8 was waiting. Hitch and I were in the front row. So everyone who came in recognized him. The plane was full and everyone was in their seats when the stewardess said, "There is a delay. Everyone gets a free drink."

Hitch couldn't just sip a drink. He up and chugged it. So half an hour goes by, and they serve another drink. Finally the stewardess tells us we don't have a full crew yet. So for fifty minutes we're sitting there. Finally the crew arrived, and they all saw Hitch. They made no apologies and began to taxi onto the runway. Then they stopped and we heard a voice come over the intercom sounding like Hitch, "Good evening, this is your pilot speaking!" The whole plane roared with laughter and Hitch gave a funny little grin.

You have told us much about Hitch and your work with him. What would you say about his trusted and trusty wife, who seemed always to be helping quietly in the background, from script to final cut?

Bumstead: When Hitch died, I went to the funeral and shortly after, Alma passed away. She was wonderful. If there were ever any problems on any film, Alma would come in, look it over, and help find a solution.

Universal Studios, Robert Mulligan, and *To Kill a Mockingbird*

Once I'm on a picture, I get lost in it.
HENRY BUMSTEAD

Henry Bumstead was very surprised when he won the Oscar for Robert Mulligan's *To Kill a Mockingbird*. Often the cast and crew of a film know whether it will be a big hit when they are working on it. But according to Bumstead, with *To Kill a Mockingbird*, "The studio thought it was slow and didn't know what they would do with it. They weren't sure anyone would really be interested in it when they previewed it. Then they realized they had a hit!" Part of that surprise comes, of course, from the kind of studio Universal had always been, as we shall explain.

The road to Bumstead's first Oscar, however, which we trace in this chapter, was a journey that took him from Paramount to Universal Studios and to five pictures made with director Robert Mulligan: *The Great Impostor* (1961), *Come September* (1961), *The Spiral Road* (1962), *To Kill a Mockingbird* (1962), and *Same Time, Next Year* (1978).

MAKING THE SWITCH TO UNIVERSAL

In 1960 there was a long actors' strike in Hollywood, and Bumstead found Universal courting him since Paramount had not signed the new agreement and there was no work going on. "I had two children in out-of-state universities at the time, and the bills were coming in," Bummy adds. Universal called him to work on Marlon Brando's film, *The Ugly*

American, being shot in Bangkok. Bumstead was accepted for the job, but the original art director decided at last that he could do it.

Thus his first Universal picture was *The Great Impostor* (1961), directed by Robert Mulligan and produced by Robert Arthur, which Bumstead calls "a great experience."[1] Paramount tried to get him back with an offer to work in Africa with John Wayne on *Hatari,* but Bumstead's back was giving him enough trouble that he opted for signing a four-picture deal at Universal, and that finally became a twenty-three-year career at Universal!

Founded by Carl Laemmle, an East European Jew, like so many of the early studio heads, early Universal Studios helped shape the whole concept of what a Hollywood studio was to become: an economic system for packaging films and talent to produce a steady stream of films. Famous producers associated with Universal included Irving Thalberg. After numerous changes in the market and filmmaking in general, Carl Laemmle Jr. led the studio successfully out of the Depression with westerns and also finely made horror films such as *Frankenstein, The Mummy,* and *The Invisible Man* (Schatz 228). By the mid-1930s, however, Universal was doing well in comedy with hits like *My Man Godfrey* and with stars such as Deanna Durbin. Through the 1940s and 1950s Universal made low-budget but successful entertainment, including Abbott and Costello as well as Ma and Pa Kettle movies; it also broke into television production, creating MCA, which took over supporting hits such as *I Love Lucy* (Schatz 475). Production designer Robert Boyle summarizes his take on Universal as what he called "one of the smaller studios" this way: "You could never depend on them being in any one place at any one time" (LoBrutto 6), a nod to an almost shotgun approach to a variety of genres and styles rather than specializing in any one area. And yet, according to Heisner's *Hollywood Art,* Universal employed some of the best art/production designers in Hollywood: Charles D. Hall, Jack Otterson, John B. Goodman, Albert D'Agostino, and the man Bumstead who came to work for, Alex Golitzen, who was head of the art department at that time (275). Golitzen was a Russian who left the Soviet Union at age sixteen and joined MGM in 1933 as an illustrator. He won an Oscar for *The Phantom of the Opera* (1943) and went on to be the art and production director for many memorable films, working with Hitchcock on *Foreign Correspondent* (1940), Orson Welles on *Touch of Evil* (1958), Fritz Lang on *Scarlet Street* (1945), and Stanley Kubrick on *Spartacus* (1960).

But by the time Bumstead came to work for Universal in 1960, the studio

A dashing Bumstead in Rome working on Come September *(1961).*
Courtesy of Henry Bumstead.

era was, as Thomas Schatz has explained, basically over, for with the rise of television a new age of "diversification and conglomeration" (481) had begun. What Universal had become good at doing over the years, however, was working with independent directors or companies for more "quality" films. Thus we see that among Bumstead's films for Universal are two for

1961   *The Great Impostor* (Robert Mulligan)
        Come September (Robert Mulligan)
1962   *The Spiral Road* (Robert Mulligan)
        To Kill a Mockingbird (Robert Mulligan)
1963   *A Gathering of Eagles* (Delbert Mann)
1964   *Bullet for a Bad Man* (R. G. Springsteen)
        The Brass Bottle (Harry Keller)
1965   *The War Lord* (Franklin Shaffner)
1966   *Beau Geste* (Douglas Hayes)
        Blindfold (Phillip Dunne)
        Gunpoint (Earl Bellamy)
1967   *Banning* (Ron Winston)
        Tobruk (Arthur Hiller)
1968   *The Secret War of Harry Frigg* (Jack Smight)
        What's So Bad about Feeling Good? (George Seaton)
1969   *Topaz* (Alfred Hitchcock)
        Tell Them Willie Boy Is Here (Abraham Polonsky)
        A Man Called Gannon (Jim Goldstone)
1970   *The Movie Murderer* (Boris Sagal)
        McCloud, Who Killed Miss USA (Richard Colla)
1971   *Raid on Rommel* (Henry Hathaway)
        One More Train to Rob (Andrew McLaglen)
1972   *Slaughterhouse-Five* (George Roy Hill)
        Joe Kidd (John Sturges)
        The Adventures of Nick Carter (Paul Krasny)
        The Victim (H. Daugherty)
1973   *Showdown* (George Seaton)
        The Sting (George Roy Hill)
1974   *Honky Tonk* (Don Taylor)
        The Front Page (Billy Wilder)
1975   *The Great Waldo Pepper* (George Roy Hill)
1976   *Family Plot* (Alfred Hitchcock)
1977   *Rollercoaster* (Jim Goldstone)
        Slap Shot (George Roy Hill)
1978   *Same Time Next Year* (Robert Mulligan)
        House Calls (Howard Zieff)
1979   *The Concorde (Airport 79)* (David Rich)
1980   *Smokey and the Bandit II* (Hal Needham)
1986   *Psycho III* (Anthony Perkins)
1990   *Ghost Dad* (Sidney Poitier)
1991   *Cape Fear* (Martin Scorcese)

Hitchcock, four for George Roy Hill, and one for Billy Wilder, to mention but three important directors who worked for several studios, depending on the project.

According to Bumstead, there was a feeling in the industry at the time that Universal went for the cheaper productions of "tits and sand" films, as they were called; but in 1959 when Universal released the very popular *Pillow Talk* with Doris Day and Rock Hudson, the studio began to pay more attention to quality projects. Forty-one pictures and two Oscars later, Bumstead still has high regard for this studio. So how was the switch from one studio to another—or, really, from one entire world to another? Bumstead's answer is quite simple: "Once I'm on a picture, I get lost in it!" (Ettedgui 20).

WORKING ON ROBERT MULLIGAN'S FILMS: YOUNG PEOPLE UNDER EMOTIONAL STRESS

Bumstead completed five films with Robert Mulligan, including *To Kill a Mockingbird*, which won him his first Oscar for production design. Rather than cover all of Bummy's films at Universal in one chapter, we are here focusing on the Mulligan films, particularly *To Kill a Mockingbird*. Other Universal films will be covered in the remaining chapters, and I discussed Bumstead's Universal films for Hitchcock: *Topaz* and *Family Plot* in the previous chapter.

Mulligan had broken into film with the impressive *Fear Strikes Out* (1957), in which a young Anthony Perkins plays baseball star Jimmy Piersall, who was afflicted with mental illness. While Mulligan went on to try other genres, as we shall see, this sense of following "young people under emotional stress" became his strongest talent in a thirty-five-year career (Thomson 530). In line with this theme, *To Kill a Mockingbird* as a book and as a film has been a lasting classic, in large part because of its ability to capture the stress of prejudice as it affects children. Similarly, Mulligan returned to this theme in 1991 in his memorable story of a young girl coming of age in a small Louisiana town in the 1950s, *Man in the Moon*, with Reese Witherspoon as the girl and Sam Waterston as her father.

And what was it like to have Bumstead working with and for Milligan? "Making a movie with Bummy," comments Mulligan, "was always a pleasure because it was like going to work with a good friend who also had a fine, artistic eye, who shared your vision, and who knew infinitely more about the practical, nuts-and-bolts business of putting a story on camera than you did" (personal letter, October 4, 2001). Furthermore, according to Mulligan, "Everything he designed served the movie. He knew how to visually bring it to life."

Production Design for a Professional Pretender:
The Great Impostor
The Great Impostor (1961); *directed by Robert Mulligan; produced by Robert Arthur; written by Liam O'Brien from the book by Robert Crichton; cinematography by Robert Burks. Cast: Tony Curtis, Raymond Massey, Karl Malden, Edmond O'Brien, Gary Merrill, and John Blackman.*

Based on the true story of one Ferdinand Demara, who carried out an unbelievable series of false identities, ranging from a Harvard professor and a navy surgeon to a prison warden, a Catholic monk, a schoolteacher, and many others, *The Great Impostor* caught America's attention as a book and as a movie. Mulligan hits an uneven tone, going for pure farce in some scenes, such as the one in which he pulls the tooth of a navy commander after comically paralyzing him with novocaine, to real tension and emotion as Demara talks down a hardened criminal in a prison fight sequence.

In short, there were a lot of very different sets to construct. But in moving over to Universal, Bumstead began this new phase of his career working under a great advantage: that most important individual for any production designer on a film, the cinematographer, was his friend Robert Burks, with whom he had already worked on *Vertigo*, *The Man Who Knew Too Much*, and *The Vagabond King*.

Bummy laughs when he remembers jumping into work in the same way he was used to at Paramount. "I completely storyboarded and sketched out the film and brought it all to Alex Golitzen, head of the Universal art department, after one week on the job. He couldn't believe I had done so much work, because that just wasn't the way they worked at Universal!"

The film, structured as a flashback tracing Demara's life, was a demanding one in terms of the number of sets. Demara had many "lives," and each life required several sets: an island in the beginning where he is arrested for being a schoolteacher, then poor streets and houses reflecting his impoverished childhood, a Catholic school that he attends as a young boy until he is thrown out, military camps for his army career, a local prison, and

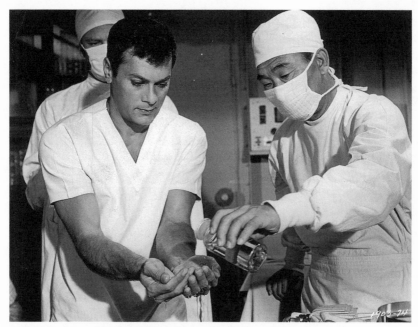

Tony Curtis pretending to be a doctor in The Great Impostor.
Copyright © 1961 by Universal-International.

Rock Hudson and Sandra Dee in an Italian villa in Come September.
Copyright © 1960 by Universal Pictures Company, Inc.

then a much larger prison where he becomes a warden, then a Catholic monastery, on-board ship interiors for his time in the navy, medical schools where as he "trains" to become the doctor he is not, and many more.[2]

But Bumstead, who had been well trained at Paramount to construct many sets on the studio lot so efficiently, has no memory of any trouble. There was one difficult day, however. "I was arrested one day on a second-unit location shoot along the California coast," he laughs, remembering the incident. The police were asking for a permit that he didn't know about. "I told them I was just the production designer, but that didn't stop them from taking me in to see the chief of police for a few hours until the studio cleared it all up!"

Bumstead says that from the beginning he liked Mulligan and recognized how talented he was, and he felt that their working relationship went very well. Mulligan, I think, felt likewise. He states: "Bummy never flaunted his knowledge or experience or brought attention to himself. That's not in his nature. But any director, with his eyes open, quickly noticed that the sets and everything related to that part of the production worked. And worked easily. All the practical details had been meticulously thought out and prepared for a director to use. Bummy had simply done his work as usual. I like to think that as a young director, I caught on quickly to how much he helped me do my job—and then learned a little more from him over the years" (October 4, 2001).

"A Good-Looking Picture": *Come September*

Come September *(1961); directed by Robert Mulligan; produced by Robert Arthur; written by Stanley Shapiro and Maurice Richlin; cinematography by William Daniels. Cast: Rock Hudson, Gina Lollobrigida, Sandra Dee, Bobby Darin, Joel Grey, Walter Slezak, and Rosanna Rory.*

Long before the frothy generational-gap comedies such as *Clueless*, there were the beginnings of 1960s youth culture comedy in a film such as *Come September*. Hip teens Bobby Darin and Sandra Dee have to put up with "old-timers" Rock Hudson and Gina Lollobrigida in this amusing romantic farce set in Italy and entirely filmed there. In this breezy comedy, New York businessman Hudson finds his Riviera villa overrun by teenagers, including Darin and Dee, and almost loses his Italian love (Lollobrigida) until he comes up with "the plan."

Bumstead has very pleasant memories of working on this one, especially doing exteriors and interiors in Europe. The photo of Bummy in Italy in this chapter certainly reflects his pleasure at that time in his career. According to Bumstead, the film was "a very funny picture with Rock Hudson, Bobby Darin, Sandra Dee, and Gina Lollobrigida. I did a marvelous interior of a villa for that film! All with Italian help, for I had nobody from Hollywood with me."

Convincing Sets and "Hilariously Miscast": *The Spiral Road*
The Spiral Road (1962); directed by Robert Mulligan; produced by Robert Arthur; written by John Lee Mahin and Neil Paterson from the novel by Jan de Hartog; cinematography by Russell Harlan. Cast: Rock Hudson, Burl Ives, Gena Rowlands, Geoffrey Keen, and Will Kuluva.

A jungle drama in Java about "love, leprosy and lunacy" (Maltin 1289), *The Spiral Road* pleased few critics, with one calling it "hilariously miscast" (Halliwell 1007). Nevertheless, it was a demanding assignment for Bumstead, for it meant finding a location to look like "Java" since so much of the film depends on exterior scenes and Javanese. Bumstead remembers doing a location search and coming up with Dutch Guiana, which has subsequently become Suriname, a republic on the north coast of South America complete with jungles, a large native population, and a very mixed overall population—37 percent Hindustani, 31 percent Creole, and 15 percent Javanese from Alanae.

"We were there about a month at least," Bumstead remembers. "And it was very *hot* and humid!" The cast and crew stayed in the capital city of Paramaribo in a primitive hotel with no windows, and he built the entire native villages in the bush with local labor. Quite a bit of construction was done around the Suriname River as well. "It was not an easy place to build sets, but all went well," he states, "for there really were snakes and rats everywhere. We even drove over a large boa constrictor that was clear across the road, but it didn't hurt him!"

During those sleepless nights in Suriname after a hard day's work, Bumstead must have thought that his quarters on location work around Tokyo on a film such as *The Bridges at Toko-Ri* were absolutely luxurious!

If critics found the overall drama of the film somewhat flat, Bumstead's sets nevertheless are very strong. Again the emphasis is on realism and attention to detail, including hotel scenes with banquets and dances, medical centers with the ever-present ceiling fans, jungle villages, and the jungle

Burl Ives (seated, left) and Rock Hudson (center) sweating in the jungle in The Spiral Road *(1962). Copyright © 1962 by Universal-International.*

itself. The scene with a dramatic fire that burns down the whole village was filmed in the village built in Suriname.

Thus during his first two years at Universal, Bumstead had ranged from the beauties of the Italian Riviera to the hardships of South American jungles and everything in between in terms of styles, buildings, and locations. Little did he know that a complete studio film representing the Deep South would lead him to his first Oscar.

Real Collard Greens and Studio Sets: *To Kill a Mockingbird*

To Kill a Mockingbird (1962); *directed by Robert Mulligan; produced by Alan Pakula; written by Horton Foote from the novel by Harper Lee; cinematography by Russell Harlan. Cast: Gregory Peck, Mary Badham, Philip Alford, John Megna, Frank Overton, Rosemary Murphy, Ruth White, Brock Peters, and Robert Duvall.*

Harper Lee's 1960 semiautobiographical novel *To Kill a Mockingbird* won the coveted Pulitzer Prize in 1961 and a strong readership around the world, becoming required reading in schools everywhere.

Building on the complexity of life in a small Alabama town in the early 1930s, much in the tradition of other great Southern writers such as William Faulkner and Eudora Welty, Lee in her only novel tells the story of a small-town Southern lawyer Atticus Finch, who takes on the case of Tom Robinson, a poor black man charged with raping a white girl. Finch then holds firm against much pressure from those around him as the case goes to trial. What engages us immediately is not the central issue of racial politics in the South but a coming-of-age story of Atticus's seven-year-old daughter, Scout, who is the narrator. It is through her eyes and those of her brother, Jem, that we experience all that is happening, as they interact with a caring father, grieve their deceased mother, and deal not only with prejudice but with coming to know Boo Radley, a reclusive, eccentric neighbor who everyone judges is "crazy."

The message of the book and the film is one of tolerance and love and their power to destroy stereotypes and prejudice. Atticus tells his tomboy daughter, as they sit on the front porch swing after she has had a hard day at school, that in judging people, "you never know someone until you step inside their skin and walk around a little."

The film version of the novel may have begun as just another adaptation of a popular novel. And surely there must have been some studio concern for a story about racial conflict at that time, as integration was such a movement and Hollywood has traditionally steered away from politically sensitive films. But Mulligan and producer Alan Pakula had a clear desire to "push the envelope" a bit, and how better to do so than in a story that embraces the whole family and is told through the eyes of a young girl too young even to be physically "coming of age"?

We are focusing on Bumstead's Oscar-winning production design, but the whole film was blessed, starting with the excellent writing by Horton Foote, which won him an Oscar for adaptation. The casting could not have been better either, beginning with Gregory Peck in the role of Atticus, which brought the actor his only Oscar. Peck had played strong roles before, but the film that most closely resembles his fine performance here is Elia Kazan's 1947 film *Gentleman's Agreement*, in which he plays a journalist pretending to be Jewish to discover how very real anti-Semitism is. Child actors can run the risk of being too cute in a Shirley Temple kind of way, but young Mary Badham was nominated for an Oscar for her spunky but realistic performance as a young girl torn in many directions. Similarly, the portrayal of blacks on screen has often run the risk of falling into stereotypes, but Brock Peters touches us deeply with the pain he has suffered and conveys. Finally, Robert Duvall in his first role is amazing in his wordless performance as Boo Radley, the "spook" down the street whom everyone mistreats because he is "different."

Robert Mulligan deserved his Oscar nomination for direction. For in bringing out the performances and balancing the tone of the film between a domestic drama and a social film, Mulligan succeeded in never letting the film become too much of a Frank Capra kind of *Mr. Smith Goes to Washington* victory or a Southern Gothic horror story on the other end. In addition, the film was nominated for Best Picture, and Elmer Bernstein and Russell Harlan received nominations for best original score and for black-and-white cinematography, respectively.

This film, with Bumstead's richly deserved Oscar-winning work, can be held up as one of the last studio-centered productions since it was so completely shot within the confines of Universal. There is a note of irony, therefore, in Bumstead's receiving his first Oscar for a film that is so heavily studio-centered when he was already making the transition to the new Hollywood trend toward shooting a lot on location, as seen in a film like *The Spiral Road*, shot the same year. Bumstead inhabited both worlds and performed brilliantly in each.

Bumstead's re-creation of the houses and the Alabama town in *To Kill a Mockingbird* were so realistic that he was frequently asked where the film was shot. He delights in answering, "Right here in Los Angeles, on the Universal lot!" Because of an amazing attention to detail—tire swings hanging from trees, broken brick supports on the house, and swings on porches—we feel we are in small-town Alabama in the 1930s, and we can almost smell the collard greens out back. Realism, therefore, is once more a trademark of Bumstead's accomplishment.

Take one small detail on the construction of the house: the house is shown to be resting on the kind of brick support columns that separate the house from the ground, creating not only a crawl space below but also protection from low flooding. A lesser art designer might have simply done a wooden house and draped Spanish moss on a tree in front. But Bumstead, with his thorough research, re-created a Southern town down to the last detail.

I interviewed Bummy about *To Kill a Mockingbird* as we watched it together again in his San Marino home. What is immediately apparent is how attentive he is to the lighting on a set, for he comments on what a

The design for the street in To Kill a Mockingbird. *Courtesy of Henry Bumstead.*

Mary Badham as Scout in To Kill a Mockingbird.
Copyright © 1962 by Universal Pictures Company, Inc.

Bumstead's attention to detail: the children seen through an old tire swing in
To Kill a Mockingbird. *Copyright © 1962 by Universal Pictures Company, Inc.*

splendid a job Russell Harlan and the lighting crew did on the night scenes and how well they worked the play of shadow and light for the daytime sequences.

But once more Mulligan turns a spotlight on Bummy, suggesting that his professionalism and personality inspire and influence all around him. "An added bonus to working with Bummy," he remarks, "was not only being exposed to his dedication and his passion for his work, but his genuine, open-hearted love for making movies is infectious. And so is his easygoing, friendly nature. All of that is intact and active still today. He hasn't changed a bit" (October 4, 2001).

Do you have an idea why Mulligan decided to shoot the film in black and white?
Bumstead: Not really, but the project was perfect for black and white.
What did you do for research on this film?
Bumstead: Alan Pakula, the producer who died so tragically recently, sent me down to meet Harper Lee in Alabama.[3] She really showed me everything. She drove me all around, and after about three or four hours she said to me, "Are you a camel?" And I said, "What do you mean?" And she said, "Don't you ever go to the bathroom?" I didn't know what a collard green was, being from California, so she took me between two old houses and there was an old lady out there. Working in her garden. She introduced me to the lady and said, "This gentleman is from Hollywood and he doesn't know what a collard green is!" The next day there was an article in the paper about the Hollywood art director in town who doesn't know collard greens!

I did get a lot of wonderful research done in Alabama. And so when they were moving a lot of houses in Los Angeles to make way for the freeway, we bought three or four of them and remodeled them. That saved the studio a lot of money. We also had to build many of the trees, especially the one with the knothole by Boo Radley's house.
You built trees?
Bumstead: Yes! You take part of a real tree, add some plaster and all, and shape it to what you want it to be. I had a great cameraman, Russell Harlan. We did continuity drawings [storyboards] based on Mulligan's rehearsals, and I think they were a great help to all the crew.
What has happened to Mary Badham, who played Scout?
Bumstead: She's married and has children. But you know, her brother is

the director John Badham, who graduated from Yale and is a wonderful director.

Were you surprised by the Oscar?

Bumstead: Very!! At the time, Hollywood still gave two Oscars for art direction, one for black and white and one for color. And I won the black and white.

Bumstead does not articulate any guiding overall plans he had in designing the sets and working with the lighting crews and cinematographer Russell Harlan. But a closer look at the film reveals, whether it was intended or not, a rhythm and guiding theme to the production design of *To Kill a Mockingbird*. There are five main physical spaces in the film:

1. Atticus's home (exterior and interior)
2. the street where they live, including the other houses such as Boo Radley's (and a few others streets as well)
3. the home of the black family in the woods
4. the woods themselves
5. the courtroom where the trial takes place

A few other locations exist, of course, but in general a good 60 percent of the story takes place in public space, outside the home. The story's center, of course, is within the family in the private space of the home, and this is captured in very simple and light colors and designs.

There is nothing fancy about Atticus's home, which is as direct and "honest" as he is. There are no suspicious shadows, no hidden corners. There is a brightly lit quality to most of these scenes, and Bumstead has given us a straightforward home with a wooden table and chairs in the kitchen for breakfast, a pleasant dining room, and simple bedrooms. There is no fancy ornamentation like we saw in the ranch mansion in *The Furies*, for instance.

Therefore, the set helps us appreciate the clarity and honesty of this family of three who are in many ways pitted against the rest of the community.

Visually the set and lighting represent this, for so many of the street scenes are at night, and Bumstead's street with its fences and trees sets up a complex web of shadows suggestive of the complexity of the community as well.

In high contrast the courtroom is huge and brightly lit. Of course the

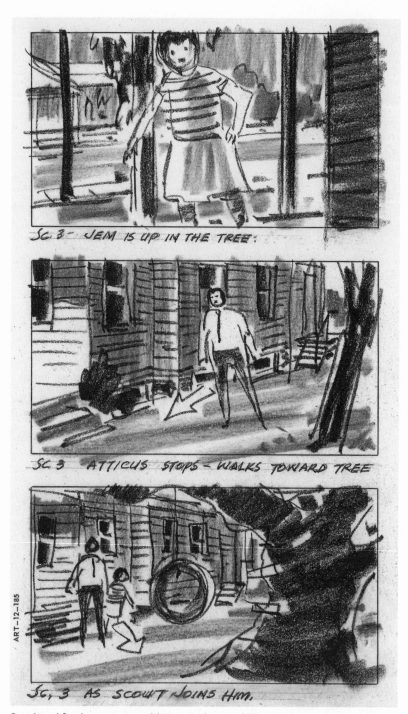

SC. 3 - JEM IS UP IN THE TREE.

SC. 3 ATTICUS STOPS - WALKS TOWARD TREE

ART—12—185

SC. 3 AS SCOUT JOINS HIM.

Storyboard for the tree scene with Jem, Atticus, and Scout in To Kill a Mockingbird. *Courtesy of Henry Bumstead.*

SC.3 HIGH ANGLE- ATTICUS CALLS TO JEM. TO
COME DOWN

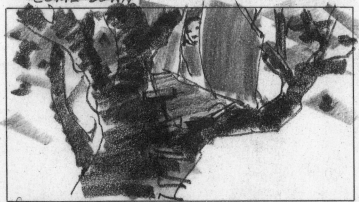

SC.3. JEM LOOKS OUT

SC.3. ATTICUS AND SCOUT HEAD TOWARD
BACK PORCH.

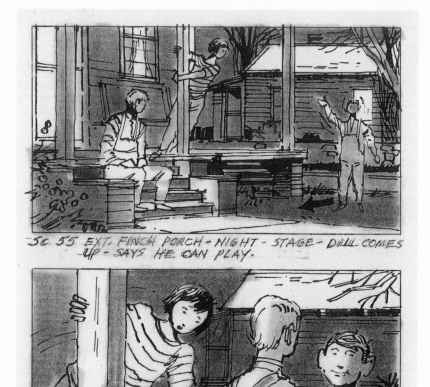

Inside storyboard panel 1: SC. 55 EXT. FINCH PORCH - NIGHT - STAGE - DILL COMES UP - SAYS HE CAN PLAY.

Inside storyboard panel 2: SC. 55 EXT. FINCH PORCH - NIGHT - STAGE - CHILDREN DECIDE TO GO FOR WALK - EXIT.

Drawing of porch activity with the children in To Kill A Mockingbird.
Courtesy of Henry Bumstead.

"light" is supposedly reflective of the clarity of the law being discussed "off the street" and away from such shadows, moral and real, reflected there. Thus the crushing emotional effect when the jury returns a guilty verdict after hearing the less than convincing evidence put forward by the prosecution.

Once more we see that what is at the center of film production design is not simply building sets or adapting locations, but a craft, as production designer Robert Boyle says, of "interpreting the film" (LoBrutto 16). The

Radley's shack in To Kill A Mockingbird.

production design is an interpretation of the emotion, tone, and meaning of the film.

On so many levels, Bumstead's sets for *To Kill a Mockingbird* convince us, as I have suggested, that like Atticus and his children, we too are involved in a complex moral situation that needs the loving clarity that the Finch home reflects. Mulligan still has very fond memories of what Bumstead accomplished for him and the pleasure it was to work together. As he puts it, "One thing is certain: there's no better companion to go off and shoot a film with than Henry 'Bummy' Bumstead" (personal letter, October 4, 2001).

Working with George Roy Hill
From Dresden to Venice and Everywhere in Between

I'm interested in characters who have illusions.
GEORGE ROY HILL

The Sting (1973) was to be Bumstead's second Oscar-winning film and the second of eight films made with director George Roy Hill. His other projects with Hill included *Slaughterhouse-Five* (1972), *The Great Waldo Pepper* (1975), *Slap Shot* (1977), *A Little Romance* (1979), *The World According to Garp* (1982), *The Little Drummer Girl* (1984), and Hill's final film, *Funny Farm* (1988).

There is always a sense of respect and affection for Hill when Bummy speaks of his work for "George," as he always refers to this director, who refused to stick to a single genre or style. Thus working with George Roy Hill was quite a different experience than working for Hitchcock, for instance. For while Hitchcock was the master of suspense and worked a fairly consistent territory of storytelling and tone in each of his films, Hill was extremely eclectic in his tastes and shied away from staying with any set pattern, even after a success such as *Butch Cassidy and the Sundance Kid*.

Before Bumstead came on board as Hill's production designer on *Slaughterhouse-Five*, Hill had six features under his belt, each in a different genre: *Period of Adjustment* (1962) was an adaptation of a Tennessee Williams play, *Toys in the Attic* (1963) was based on a Lillian Hellman play, *The World of Henry Orient* (1964) was a light comedy featuring Peter Sellers, *Hawaii* (1966) was a sprawling epic based on the James Michener novel, *Thoroughly Modern Millie* (1967) was a tour de force farce building on elements and clichés from romantic comedy, silent comedy, musicals, Cinderella-type fairy tales, and more (Horton, *The Films of George Roy Hill*, 59). And *Butch Cassidy and the Sundance Kid* took the dying genre of the western and gave it new life as a comic and at times touching buddy road film based on William Goldman's brilliant original script and Paul Newman and Robert Redford's playful on-screen chemistry as two likeable rogues who do not understand that the West is changing so rapidly that it is leaving them behind.

Was there a common thread in Hill's work that Bumstead recognized, if not immediately, then after working with him on several films? The answer is "yes," and in fact several characteristics emerge as part of "the George Roy Hill touch." These would include the courage to take on difficult or unusual material and to take chances with it. How do you turn a sprawling epic like *Hawaii,* for instance, into any kind of coherent film that plays under three hours? Or how do you dare start your career with two black-and-white films based on stage plays without seeming boring or pretentious?

Hill's protagonists share some characteristics. "I'm interested in characters who have illusions," states Hill (ibid. 3). "An awful lot of my characters and a lot of the characters I am drawn to are people who have ideals that are unreachable because they are glamorized ideals, and they do not really apply to regular life. In fact, when one applies these ideals to regular life, it all falls apart," states the director, who graduated from Yale and began in theater before moving to film in the early 1960s.

Bumstead couldn't have joined Hill at a better time. Both were working at the top of their form, as Hill was coming off the success of *Butch Cassidy* and Bummy was bringing such a rich résumé of splendid films with him to what became one of his favorite projects, *Slaughterhouse-Five.* Each Hill project was, as I have suggested, a unique challenge for Bumstead, but we shall focus on *Slaughterhouse-Five* and *The Sting.*

You made the point that Hitch didn't always need to see the set. He trusted you. What about George Roy Hill?
Bumstead: Yes, he would look at them, but this is how I worked with George, especially when I did *The Little Drummer Girl,* which we shot in five or six countries. I would shoot color stills on five or six locations

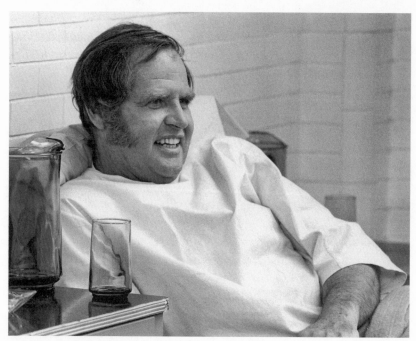

Bummy as actor playing Rosewater in Slaughterhouse-Five.
Courtesy of Henry Bumstead.

and then mount the photographs on cardboard and come back to show George. I would show him a number of locations for each set, and he would pick the one or ones he wanted to see. So when we scouted the location, we only scouted the ones we wanted to see. This saved lots of time, so George could concentrate on the story and casting. In fact, Hill said to me in the office one day on *Little Drummer Girl,* "Thanks a lot, Bummy, you have saved me a lot of time." I more or less work that way with others, including Clint too. But Clint is even more that way. He will just say, "It's okay, Bummy," and I will point out that he hasn't really seen what I've done. And he will say, "But you know what I like and want, so it's not a problem."

"IT WAS A GOOD-LOOKING PICTURE":
SLAUGHTERHOUSE-FIVE

Slaughterhouse-Five (1972); directed by George Roy Hill; produced by Paul Monash for Universal; written by Stephen Geller from the novel by Kurt Vonnegut Jr.; cinematography by Miroslav Ondricek. Cast: Michael Sacks, Ron Leibman, Valerie Perrine, Eugene Roche, Sharon Gans, and Friedrich Ledebur.

Slaughterhouse-Five had been an extremely popular novel by Kurt Vonnegut Jr. that was based on the author's actual experiences surrounding the firebombing of the city of Dresden near the end of World War II. Shot while the Vietnam War was still raging, Vonnegut's darkly satiric tale was viewed as both a strong antiwar statement and a broad send-up of postwar American culture with a hilarious sci-fi element thrown in, too.

Thus Bumstead's challenge was to create a satirical look to contemporary American culture, to come up with an exaggerated "futuristic" world on another planet (Tralfamadore), and, most difficult of all, to re-create the city of Dresden before, during, and after the Allied firebombing attack. A closer look may help explain why Bumstead often says, "I really feel I should have gotten an Oscar for this one rather than *The Sting!*" And indeed it is hard to argue with his assessment.

How did you wind up working with George Roy Hill?
Bumstead: I did *Tell Them Willy Boy Is Here* (1969) with Robert Redford, and the cinematographer on that was Conrad Hall. I remember Conrad was talking on the set about going over to Twentieth Century Fox to do *Butch Cassidy and the Sundance Kid*. Perhaps it was Conrad who mentioned me to Hill. Or as Robert Crawford told me—he was one of Hill's producers—it may have been a production manager, Ernie Wehmeyer, who said to George he should meet me, but I don't know for sure.

Either way, I was vacationing in Oregon with my family when I got a call to come down to the studio because George Roy Hill wanted to meet me. So I came down, we had a nice chat, and he asked if I would like to do *Slaughterhouse-Five*. He made it clear we couldn't do the film in the States for a reasonable budget. So I was naturally nervous, as I was with Hitchcock, because it would mean working overseas in a country still under communism.

When I signed on, we went on a scouting tour, and we were particularly looking for areas that had been hit by earthquakes in hopes there would be ruins we could use for the bombed-out look of Dresden after the war. We went to Yugoslavia, Romania, and Budapest, Hungary, and we finally ended up in Prague, which had recently been taken over by the Russians. Fortunately we found a town called Most, which was being demolished by the government in order to get at the coal underneath.

I was having back trouble at the time, and George had had back trouble as well, so he was very understanding. We needed the Czech government's approval to use the town, and I was surprised they gave it to us. I must say, I was surprised a studio like Universal would make a picture such as *Slaughterhouse-Five*! Jennings Lang, one of the producers, really wanted to see this film made.

We came back to California, and I blocked out all the sets and made a budget. We then returned to Prague and Barrandov Studios and discussed set-by-set construction, locations, extras, and everything else. The Czechs gave us their budget, and it was surprisingly low. There were some things they couldn't do, of course, including Tralfamadore and the American locations. I was there alone in October and November, looking for locations. About Christmas, Ray Gosnell, the first assistant, joined me, and it was really cold, even in the hotel. They would hang blankets over the windows to keep the cold out! It was all pretty primitive—the hotel still had pull-chain toilets and just a bathtub, no showers. It's all changed now, of course.

As I remember, the set we built for the bombing of Dresden took five or six months to do, and it was so cold you had to heat the paint— you couldn't believe it. Every time I went to the set, I would take some brandy to the workers! They loved it *and* me! It was a tough show. But everything went well over there. Then we came home and shot in Minneapolis, where George was raised as a child, for the "contemporary" American scenes in the book. The cameraman was great, too: Miroslav Ondricek, who later worked on *The World According to Garp*.

I look back now, and I think here's what really sold George on me. In the script Billy Pilgrim was killed on a stage, but I found this wonderful building seven or eight stories high, with an atrium that was perfect, and we were able to hide all the Tralfamadorians around the balconies. It was so much better and [more] mysterious than if we had shot in a theater, which would probably have been almost impossible to do and get the effect created by the novel and the script.

I got along great with George. We had a few misunderstandings, but we worked them out and became very good friends.

Do you have Slaughterhouse-Five *drawings?*

Bumstead: No, but we did a lot of drawing and designing. We were lucky at the time because there were only one or two good crews in Prague then, and we had the best. Paint wasn't good there, and I'll never forget our work on the scenes for the burning of Dresden. I had a talented assistant, Bob Kulic, who didn't speak English, so I would make drawings of what I needed, and then he would make drawings for the Czech crew. For instance, on my first trip to France I didn't speak French, so I drew a glass of water and the waiter brought me some! That's how we communicated! It was eight or nine months from scouting for *Slaughterhouse-Five* to finishing the shooting.

Let's summarize the whole film briefly. *Slaughterhouse-Five* "plays" with three different time periods: the World War II sequences leading up to the firebombing of Dresden, the present in the 1960s in America, and an imagined future in which Billy Pilgrim winds up mating with Montana Wildhack. Bumstead had to work with all three periods, shot in three locations—the Czech Republic, Minneapolis, and Hollywood—and bring it all together so that the film had a visual consistency. (Note that "consistency" in this case emphasized constant contrasts between the time switches for a main character who was "unstuck in time," as Vonnegut and Billy both say.)

World War II

Bumstead has mentioned the sheer difficulty of the logistics of working in a foreign country in winter when English is in short supply along with other needed materials. Thus, on one level, a large "bravo!" for simply getting the job done on location in Prague with local labor.

Prague proved a brilliant choice not only because it saved money, but also because the look of this beautiful city succeeds admirably in helping us understand the loss of Dresden after the bombing. This is the part of production design that involves location choosing. Set to classical music, the montage of the American and British prisoners coming into Dresden is a masterful sequence. The play of shots between the faces of the people and the prisoners, the stunning architecture and the soldiers, all seen through Billy Pilgrim's amazed glances at this world beyond anything he has ever

Billy Pilgrim (Michael Sacks) carrying a clock through a destroyed Dresden in Slaughterhouse-Five. *Copyright © by Universal Pictures.*

known, succeeds in helping viewers grasp the enormity of the destruction that follows.

The bombed-out city is, of course, the result of Bumstead's sets — that is, his amplification and transformation of the Czech city, Most. Bummy and his crew were able to make use of the Czech government's actual destruction of the city for this important sequence, with its burning and crumbling buildings, rubble everywhere, and smoke drifting over all with snow scattered around as well. We feel the loss of Dresden keenly because of Bumstead's work.

America

Some interiors of Billy's home, for instance, were done on location and at Universal, but a lot involved location shots in the Minneapolis, Minnesota, area where director George Roy Hill had grown up. Knowing this, one feels strongly that Bumstead's choice of locations in part reflects

Bumstead's re-creation of the firebombing of Dresden in Slaughterhouse-Five, *which was shot in a town outside of Prague. Copyright © 1972 by Universal Pictures.*

Hill's effort to make Billy Pilgrim's story a more personal one for him. The Minneapolis locations also indicate that the film is not an East or West Coast story or a Southern tale either.

Contemporary sets also include the convention, the hospital, and the highways as Billy's wife races to the hospital to see Billy. Hill (and therefore Bumstead) develops these contemporary scenes more than Vonnegut does in the novel, thus adding an even more satirical edge to this tale of a simple fellow.

The "Imagined" Future on the Planet Tralfalmadore

In Vonnegut's novel the Tralfamadorans exist as space creatures, and the sci-fi element has a stronger, more involved presence than in the film. But Hill consciously cut back on all of this so that Tralfamadore is more of an ambiance, not a world of little creatures (ibid. 85). Thus Bumstead has created a wonderful transparent dome with Billy "on stage" in a bland-looking, Sears and Roebuck–like middle-class living room in space.

A voice from outside the dome (in actuality, the voice of director George Roy Hill) is the voice of a Tralfamadoran, however, thus reminding Billy that he is being observed by these unseen inhabitants of another world. Once again, Bumstead succeeds so well with extreme simplicity.

A final note on the brilliance of Dede Allen's editing and Bumstead's production design. Editing is extremely important for this story because the three time periods are constantly mixed. And the combined talents of Bumstead and Allen can be seen in cut after cut. For example, in one scene we see Billy as a little boy taking a shower at the local community pool his father has taken him to. In close-up we see the shower head beginning to pour out, and the cut is clearly a different shower head as we pull back to see that it is one being used by Billy and the American prisoners in the Nazi prison camp. I have often been impressed with how many people have told me, years after seeing the film, that such cuts are a major part of what they appreciated about the film.

THE STING: "I LIKE TO DO 'CHARACTER SETS' LIKE TO KILL A MOCKINGBIRD AND THE STING"

The Sting (1973); directed by George Roy Hill; produced by Tony Bill, Julia Phillips, and Michael Phillips for Universal; written by David S. Ward; cinematography by Robert Surtees. Cast: Robert Redford, Paul Newman, Robert Shaw, Charles Durning, Ray Walson, Eileen Brennan, and Harold Gould.

The Sting not only won Bumstead his second Oscar, but it also won George Roy Hill the award and teamed Redford and Newman for a second time. And the popularity of the film has not diminished over the years. In fact, Robert Redford puts it well when he says, "I think George's work will be seen as outstanding in years to come, and The Sting is one of the best" (ibid. 102). Rather than a sequel to Butch Cassidy and the Sundance Kid, The Sting is a strong adventure/caper film that is set in the 1930s and is more of a "father-son" tale than a buddy film. For as Hill makes clear, Newman is the old con man passing his skill on to the younger con, played by Redford (ibid. 100).

Thus while Bumstead likewise was again working with the popular duo, the emphasis was not on the world of exteriors that westerns conjure up. Rather, Bummy created many interior sets of the 1930s, including a train compartment and buildings in and around Chicago.

Sketch of Gondorff's room in The Sting. *Courtesy of Henry Bumstead.*

Sketch detail of Gondorff in The Sting. *Courtesy of Henry Bumstead.*

As Bumstead and I watched *The Sting* together, he commented on his love for Depression-period photographs as well as details of particular scenes.

What do you see as your distinctive touch in the design of The Sting?
Bumstead: I think one of the biggest contributions I made on *The Sting* was the use of color, because Hill asked me about color for such a period film. And I told him that I remembered that period as everything in

The big poker game in the speakeasy in The Sting.
Copyright © 1974 by Universal Pictures.

brown. It was the Depression. Bob Surtees, the cameraman—what a man and cameraman!—he agreed, too. So that's what gave the film that special look. I think this one element really enhanced the film. That is, aged period sets. But of course a good production designer can do any period or style, Including outer space, like my latest one, *Space Cowboys*.

Walker Evans—I referred to him often. For instance, I couldn't find a look for the opening sequence, and then one morning going to work I saw this street in Pasadena and that was it! The minute I got to the studio I called George and took him to Pasadena. And he loved it. So that location was solved because that street reminded me of Walker Evans's photographs.

Your drawings are amazing for the shadows and play of light you show. How much of any given shot is you and how much is the cinematographer?

Bumstead: Well, I work very closely with cameramen. But it is true that our drawings and storyboards do suggest the use of shadow and light as well as set design. [watching the early scenes of the film] See, the colors are wonderful, aren't they?

Newman crossing a "well-dressed" set for The Sting.
Copyright © by Universal Pictures.

On a period film, is there anything in particular you pay attention to?

Bumstead: Architecture, wardrobe, and automobiles really help create the
period. [watching a Chicago hotel scene] It's one of the oldest hotels
around [the Green Hotel in Pasadena] and a home for the aged now.
[Bumstead shows obvious interest in the play between what a building
can be used for in a film and then in real life.]

How long does it take to do a room like the one we are seeing here?

Bumstead: With construction, set dressing, et cetera, it probably took a
week. But look how well it is shot by Robert Surtees. He was quite a guy.
He had sixteen nominations for Oscars and three wins. I did *The Sting,*
The Great Waldo Pepper, and *Same Time, Next Year* with him. [watch-
ing the famous card game in the train sequence] That's all a train set on

the stage. Surtees wanted this room painted darker than the usual train colors for lighting effects. That card game is one of the great movie card games of all time.

Is it true you used a real merry-go-round in Santa Monica for this scene?

Bumstead: Yes. And this barbershop we are seeing now is a real barbershop in Chicago. [a sequence with music and no dialogue leads to the train station] Isn't it wonderful! And that's the train station in Chicago. And that's a bank in Pasadena. It's a period bank across from the Christian Science Reading Room on Colorado Boulevard. But the whorehouse is a set. [a bit later] Oh, this was a rush set, as usual. Jim Payne, the set decorator, and I worked all night with construction, paint, set dressing, et cetera, to get it ready on time. George was tickled to death.

Were you surprised The Sting *won the Oscar?*

Bumstead: I was surprised. But I did think I had a good chance. It's a thrill to win an Oscar, but the biggest thrill is afterward when you get calls from kids you went to high school with, art directors, directors, friends, and even some pilots from the aircraft carrier USS *Oriskany* where we filmed some of the sea scenes for *The Bridges at Toko-Ri*.

THE GREAT WALDO PEPPER

The Great Waldo Pepper (1975); *directed and produced by George Roy Hill for Universal; written by William Goldman from a story by George Roy Hill; cinematography by Robert Surtees. Cast: Robert Redford, Bo Svenson, Susan Sarandon, Bo Brundin, Ed Hermann, and Philip Burns.*

Of all the films he made, *The Great Waldo Pepper* is perhaps the one closest to George Roy Hill's heart for a simple reason: Hill himself was a pilot. As noted above, story credit goes to Hill on this one, and he worked closely with William Goldman to have him flesh out the story of a barnstorming pilot who is part con man and part adventuresome rouge (ibid. 126).

What the film contrasts is self-created myth and reality. In set terms, this translates as the actual locations of "Nebraska" in the story, which Bumstead scouted mostly in Kansas, and a Hollywood of the 1920s when Pepper (Robert Redford) becomes a pilot in a reenactment of World War I aerial fights with the Germans. Put even more simply, the contrast in the film is between life on the ground and the freedom of life in the air.

Bumstead's eventual use of Texas locations admirably evokes the "Ne-

Panic ensues as barnstorming pilot Robert Redford zooms by in
The Great Waldo Pepper. *Copyright © 1975 by Universal Pictures.*

braska" of Pepper's youth, and the Hollywood of the 1920s was clearly pure
fun for Bummy to work with.

What was it like to go from The Sting *to a film about planes,* The Great
   Waldo Pepper?
Bumstead: Once again, it's a character picture and a historical period picture, too. I remember choosing locations in Kansas. Winter was approaching, and all of a sudden we got word that Redford couldn't meet
   the starting date because he was running over schedule in England on
   The Great Gatsby. So we had to leave all these wonderful places I had
   found in Kansas.

   So we switched to Texas because of the weather. I had to find the
   locations all over again, which I did. And we found some good ones.
   But one scene wound up in Elgin, Texas. That's the scene where they

flew through the streets of a town. [laughs] You never realize how much overhead crap there is on American streets until you start looking for some streets a plane could fly down! A great town, Elgin, but I did have to take a few things down. We had to turn the lampposts around, for instance, with the permission of the town council. And as I remember, we built a swimming pool in their park in exchange for all they did for us! I'll never forget the day Frank Tallman [the stunt pilot] flew the plane down the street with only about eight or ten feet on either side—I was so nervous. But he did it! I still correspond with his wife, Ruth "Boots" Tallman.[1]

We had some wonderful flying scenes that got cut out. I don't know why. A lot of the film was shot on location, including a lot of interiors that we built in a hangar in San Marcos, Texas. You know, you need to do that to have "cover sets" just in case you have weather problems and you have to move inside. Oh, and I had to build a big carnival set for the film, too, where Tallman crashed into the carnival.

It was a very rainy season that year. And at one point I built a French château where the officers lived, near Piru, California. [laughs] It was funny, one morning we went out to look at the set, but to our surprise, there was no château! We found out the construction crew had not built it sturdy enough, so a big wind came up during the night and blew it all down. Tallman crashed during a landing near Piru but not on camera. He was rushed to the hospital and, thank goodness, survived. What wonderful flying scenes were done by Tallman and Frank Pine. Pine crashed, too, and had to be taken to the hospital.

SLAP SHOT

Slap Shot (1977); directed by George Roy Hill; produced by Robert J. Wunsch and Stephen Friedman for Universal; written by Nancy Dowd; cinematography by Vic Kemper. Cast: Paul Newman, Michael Ontkean, Lindsay Crouse, Jennifer Warren, Jerry Houser, and Strother Martin.

Slap Shot continues to be very much a cult film in Canada and wherever else ice hockey counts more than almost anything else. Paul Newman plays the coach of a failing bush-league pro hockey team made up of misfits and overgrown kids with sticks. On the ice and off, it's a fast-paced, farcical sports drama based on many true-life experiences of screen-

Paul Newman as the feisty coach of a losing bush-league hockey team in Slap Shot.

writer Nancy Dowd's brother. Locations, therefore, center around ice rinks, cheap bars, and on-the-road experiences of a down-and-out team. It's a film that Newman confessed he had a lot of fun making (ibid. 132).

Did you have as much fun as Newman did on this film?
Bumstead: *Slap Shot* was a tough picture. We filmed on a lot of locations, including Johnstown, Pennsylvania, and Colgate University, a beautiful college campus in upstate New York. We scouted in Canada and looked and looked and looked and finally settled on Johnstown. *Slap Shot* was so rushed. We had to change our locations time and time again according to the availability of the hockey players we had to bring in from here and there. It was very rushed! Not only that, while George was shooting, I was out elsewhere scouting for future locations.

   The company was shooting six days a week, and I was scouting future locations. Then George and I had to spend all day Sunday looking at locations I had found. So after about four Sundays of this, George turns to me and says, "I'm really getting tired of spending every Sunday with you, Bummy!" And I said, "Me too, George. I'd like to have today off for golf or something else!" But it was kind of cute of him! All we did back in the studio was a bedroom and a living room. Everything else was done on location.

Near the end of the picture, Newman lets loose with what was described by several critics at the time as one of the most obscene outbursts in American cinema up to that date.[2] Did that have any effect on your work?

Bumstead: I think the last sequence and the swear words Newman had to say, I wasn't happy with, because I had to find an interior location for him for that scene. It made me very nervous. The homes I liked were owned by little old ladies, and I couldn't have Paul saying those awful things in their homes, but luckily we did find a place, and they shot there. I was on my way home and wasn't there to see the reaction, thank goodness, so I didn't know how they reacted.

Where was the house that was finally used?

Bumstead: I can't remember, but it was near Johnstown. It is funny how many people remember this film. When I was doing *Unforgiven* in Canada, our group of four took a break after playing golf and were having a beer when the crew heard that I had done *Slap Shot*. Well, from then on, I could do no wrong! I was their hero and that was their favorite film. And it's still a cult picture. I directed some of the second unit work where their bus is traveling through the snow on the way to another game.

"ONE OF MY FAVORITE FILMS": *A LITTLE ROMANCE*
A Little Romance (1979); *directed by George Roy Hill; produced by Yves Rousset-Rouard and Robert Crawford for Warner Brothers; written by Allen Burns from the novel* E = MC², Mon Amour *by Patrick Chauvin; cinematography by Pierre William Glenn. Cast: Laurence Olivier, Diane Lane, Thelonious Bernard, Arthur Hill, Sally Kellerman, and Broderick Crawford.*

A *Little Romance* is a romantic comedy involving young teens and set in France and Italy—Paris, Verona, and, finally, Venice. By 1979 Bumstead had, of course, a lot of experience working in Europe, so he was not very worried about tackling this on-the-road romance between a teenage Diane Lane as an American girl and a young French boy, Thelonious Bernard, who had never acted before.

Laurence Olivier fades in and out of the story as a kind of fairy godfather

Laurence Olivier having a grand time bike racing in A Little Romance.
Copyright © by Orion Pictures Company.

helping to orchestrate and protect this energetic young couple. What Bumstead managed was a lot of work on location in these three cities "touching up" and working over existing locations for a film that sparkles with warmth and humor.

This was another film shot in Europe, which suggests a lot of logistic and technical problems. But it must have been easier than, say, Slaughterhouse-Five.

Bumstead: This is one of my favorite pictures. I remember I was in Paris, Verona, and Venice scouting locations for the film when George got word that Universal wouldn't do the picture. So George returned to California to get a new sponsor. It looked like we would have to cancel, and I held everything together for him while he negotiated in California. Finally Orion came through. *A Little Romance* was their first picture. I was over there a long time looking for locations. I was having back trouble again, and all those cobblestone streets were very bad for my back.

I had a talented French art director, François Delamothe, working with me. But he was very jealous of me, and I had a talented set decorator, Robert Christides, who was a great help to me. I built many sets on location, but only one in a French studio [Billancourt]. My back was getting worse and I told George I would like to go home, especially because I felt François didn't want me there. All the locations were chosen, plus the set in the studio was complete, so off I went for home and a back operation.

In Verona I took an insurance office and made it into a hotel. And I must say I'm proud that for years later when people came to Verona, they wanted to stay in that hotel, but there was no hotel! We chose locations in Venice too, of course, but then I went home before shooting began.

George likes to rehearse for a couple of weeks before a picture. So I would lay the sets out [on the floor] with different-colored tape, one set over another. And George loved to try and figure out which was which, and I must say he was very good at it!

THE WORLD ACCORDING TO GARP

The World According to Garp (1982); *directed by George Roy Hill; produced by Robert Crawford for Warner Brothers; screenplay by Steve Tesich, based on the novel by John Irving; cinematography by Mirislov Ondricek. Cast: Robin Williams, Glenn Close, Mary Beth Hurt, John Lithgow, Hume Cronyn, Jessica Tandy, and Swoosie Kurtz.*

As mentioned earlier, I met Bumstead on the set of *The World According to Garp*, so this is the one film of his on which I have had the opportunity to watch him at work over a period of several months. I begin with what is obviously clear by now: his complete grasp of the big picture and, simultaneously, his attention to detail. But there is more: what became quite impressive was his easygoing professionalism (he never seemed flustered or nervous), his seemingly endless good humor, and his readiness to make whatever adjustments or changes that were necessary for all to run smoothly or requested by Hill.

When Hill was offered *The World According to Garp* by Warner Brothers, he didn't see how such a complex novel about the life of a writer could be brought to the screen. Once Steve Tesich wrestled with the screenplay, however, and simplified the story while keeping the spirit of John Irving's novel, the project was on.

I met you on the set of The World According to Garp, *as you know, but I want to hear your view of what it was like to work on the film.*

Bumstead: Well, at that time I was working on *The Best Little Whorehouse in Texas*. George called and asked if I would work on *Garp*. "I would love to," I told him, "but I've scouted *Whorehouse* and started to build sets." George was upset with me, but I would never leave a film I was working on, and I never have. However, about a week later there was an actors' strike that shut down *Whorehouse*. So I called George and said, "I'll do it!" Of course, Universal wasn't happy I left their picture, but anyway, I was then on *Garp*.

I got things organized for Hill. What I did—and what I like to do—is rough out a lot of sets and show George. Plus I was busy looking for locations around New York, besides figuring out sets we could shoot in the Astoria Studios in Brooklyn.

It was a great film to work on for many reasons, but one of them was to meet new actors, since this was the first film for Glenn Close and John Lithgow.

The film is basically comic, but there are some strong dramatic moments as well. Could you comment on your reaction to the film?

Bumstead: One of the things I really remember was when we had gone one day for dailies and we were watching Robin Williams's death scene as he was in the helicopter pulling away from the school. A few of us were returning to our apartments in a limo, and I told George that it was a terrific scene and tears had rolled down my cheeks while watching it. George said in his typical way, "Don't listen to Bummy—he'd cry at the

The stunt crash into the home Garp wishes to buy in The World According to Garp.
Courtesy of Henry Bumstead.

opening of a supermarket." George knew I was very sentimental. And he is right. I mean, I could go to a stranger's funeral and tears would come, I'm sure. Everyone laughed and I'll always remember that—"Bummy would cry at the opening of a supermarket."

I was on location for the scene of the plane crashing into the house that Robin Williams is trying to buy. Did you build that house?

Bumstead: Absolutely. James Appleby was the pilot, and I worked with him. I built the back of Garp's house at the side of an airport runway in New Jersey and had a strong net built to stop the plane. Appleby had never done a stunt like this before, so I was very nervous and watched from the other side of the runway. Once the shot was over and all was okay, the cops wouldn't let me across the field to congratulate Appleby. But I was thrilled that it worked and Appleby was not hurt.

THE LITTLE DRUMMER GIRL

The Little Drummer Girl (1984); directed by George Roy Hill; produced by George Roy Hill, Robert Crawford, and Pat Kelley for Warner Brothers; written by Loring Mandel from the novel by John le Carré; cinematography by Wolfgang Treu. Cast: Diane Keaton, Klaus Kinski, Yorgo Voyagis, Sami Frey, and Eli Danker.

John le Carré's novel *The Little Drummer Girl* would at first seem an unlikely work for George Roy Hill to take on. Treating as it does Israeli and Palestinian conflicts in the Middle East more than twenty years before the tragic outbursts of violence during 2001–2002, le Carré's fiction asks the reader to consider some of the most difficult questions of the past and present century, for which there are no Hollywood endings or even comic-dramatic endings such as *Butch Cassidy and the Sundance Kid* and *Slaughterhouse-Five*. But if George Roy Hill had one major characteristic as a director, it was that he was eclectic and in many ways purposely tried to make each film quite different from previous works (ibid. 7).

Thus for a production designer *The Little Drummer Girl* was challenging from the beginning. For whereas *Slaughterhouse-Five* was difficult because of both the need for historical re-creation and the task of working abroad, *The Little Drummer Girl* concerns contemporary issues still very much in flux, with Hill insisting on trying to shoot as much as possible on location.

The Little Drummer Girl *was a very ambitious project, given all the foreign locations. I know you even shot in Greece and Israel, true?*

Bumstead: Our home base was Bavaria Ateuiel in Munich, Germany, and that's where we built most of the sets. We filmed exteriors and interiors in England, Germany, Israel, Beirut, Lebanon, and Greece. In Jerusalem thieves broke into my car and took everything, including 2,000 German marks, my passport, camera, everything. We were moving from country to country so fast on this film that I really needed all the stolen items. I think I had five passports during the filming because different countries wouldn't honor each other's passports. Fortunately, producer Bob Crawford had xeroxed my passport so he was able to help me get a new one quickly. In Jericho, for instance, we built a set in a Palestinian camp. We were filming a market scene, and they told us they wouldn't serve lunch on the set because they were afraid the Palestinians would

Diane Keaton in training with Palestinian freedom fighters in
The Little Drummer Girl. *Copyright © 1984 by Warner Bros. Inc.*

want to have it too. Then the Palestinian kids started tearing down our set because we were working with the Israelis. We had to get out fast. It was very scary. We were also in Beirut, Lebanon. Very scary. And we built a lot of sets in Munich, England, Israel, and Greece. It was an interesting picture but a tough job because of so many sets in so many different countries. They had a terrible time with the cast. George Roy Hill couldn't get the actors he wanted.

When we were in Beirut, I couldn't believe how much destruction had happened to that beautiful city. The war was still going on at that time. I mean, I could see explosions going on up in the hills while we were there. Very sad and scary.

I had some talented help on *The Little Drummer Girl,* including cinematographer Wolfgang Treu, art director Helmut Gassner, illustrator Gene Johnson, and set decorator Heidi Ludi—and a good construction crew.

George Roy Hill and Robert Redford sharing a laugh on the set of
The Great Waldo Pepper. Copyright © by Universal Pictures.

Funny Farm

Funny Farm (1988); directed by George Roy Hill; produced by Bruce Bodner,
Robert Crawford, and Patrick Kelley for Warner Brothers; written by Jeffrey
Boam from the novel by Jay Cronley; cinematography by Miroslav Ondricek.
Cast: Chevy Chase, Madolyn Smith-Osborne, Kevin O'Morrison, Joseph
Maher, Caris Corfman, Jack Gilpin.

Funny Farm *was George Roy Hill's last film. Was it a difficult project?*

Bumstead: I did a lot of scouting in Vermont and New Hampshire. We
found a house and farm in Grafton, Vermont. We did a lot of work on
the house, interior and exterior, to make it work. The weather was a big
factor. It was *cold*. We built a gazebo in Townshend, Vermont, on the
town square, and it still stands. I also built a restaurant there that I was
proud of, but we had to strike it after filming. We shot the whole film
on location. We found everything we needed! George didn't want this
to be just slapstick comedy. Carol Wood did a lot of continuity sketches
on this picture on very funny sequences, and Henry Larrecq, my art di-

rector, who worked on many of my films, including *The Sting,* was a great help, as usual.

And after *Funny Farm* I traveled to Rome and Florence, Italy, with George and Bob Crawford, his producer, because he wanted to do a picture, called *Winning Ugly,* about American football in Rome. The story is about American coaches coaching a ragtag team of truck drivers and lawyers and doctors. It was a good story, and we spent a month picking beautiful locations, designing sets, doing a budget, and making a schedule. Stefano Ortolani, an Italian art director, was a great help to me.

When I got back from Italy, Clint Eastwood called and wanted me to do *Unforgiven,* but I told him I was working with George, and Clint said he would wait for me a few weeks. Shortly after, George called and said the picture was off because he couldn't cast it. A few minutes later Clint called. My wife answered the phone and asked who was calling, and he said "Clint Eastwood." My wife hung up on him because she didn't believe it was Clint! I overheard the call, called back, and said I would do it. Clint got a real kick out of Lena hanging up on him.

George Roy Hill had been fighting Parkinson's disease for many years, and by then it was beginning to show. It is more than a pity, for the strong working relationship that Hill and Bummy had formed over the years in which they worked together would surely have led to even more exciting projects had Hill been able to continue.

The Eastwood Films
"Clint Does His Homework"

Clint has done so many wonderful films.
He's a great director and a lot of fun to work with.
HENRY BUMSTEAD

It's a simple fact of film history that most established directors have surrounded themselves with a trusted team of coworkers and artists whom they enjoy working with and who they know will make a big contribution to their films. But part of the pleasure of following Henry Bumstead's career is to see the variety of talented directors he has had the opportunity to work with. This final "director-centered" chapter concerns Bummy's work with Clint Eastwood. And the differences between Eastwood and the other directors with whom Bumstead has made four or more films—Alfred Hitchcock, Robert Mulligan, and George Roy Hill—far outweigh the similarities.

Bumstead has worked on nine films directed by Clint Eastwood: *High Plains Drifter* (1973), *Unforgiven* (1992), *A Perfect World* (1993), *Absolute Power* (1996), *Midnight in the Garden of Good and Evil* (1997), *True Crime* (1999), *Space Cowboys* (2000), *Blood Work* (2002), and *Mystic River* (2003). We will focus on four of them: *High Plains Drifter*, *Unforgiven*, *A Perfect World*, and *Space Cowboys*.

Eastwood as director, actor, and person is in many ways best summed up by critic/scholar David Thomson when he writes, "Clint Eastwood is among the very few Americans admired and respected at home and abroad, without qualification or irony" (221).[1] What makes Eastwood Eastwood? No simple answer is satisfactory, but William Beard has suggested that his two strong mentors in filmmaking—Sergio Leone for the so-called "spaghetti westerns" such as A *Fist Full of Dollars* (1964), *For a Few Dollars More* (1965), and *The Good, the Bad, and the Ugly* (1966) and Don Siegel for tough genre films such as *Coogan's Bluff* (1968), *Two Mules for Sister Sara* (1970), *The Beguiled* (1971), *Dirty Harry* (1971), and *Escape from Alcatraz* (1979)—embedded a strong "double vision" in Clint's vision of cinema as a filmmaker (153). From Siegel, Eastwood has learned to be "straightforward, lean, and hard hitting" (151), and, according to Beard, from Leone, Eastwood has learned to be a daring visual stylist, pushing shots to "eye-popping visual exaggerations" (152).

As a character in front of the camera, Eastwood has always held our attention as a figure who seems "too large for society" (Thompson and Hunter 113). The Eastwood figure has a dream to reach his own goals and right wrongs his own way, above and beyond the rules of society. But he does so at a price: almost always his actions mean he becomes isolated from others. As Thompson notes, Eastwood's characters seem to "suggest that good can triumph in the world only when set apart from it" (113). Thus the common motif of Eastwood as a "man with no name" riding out of "nowhere" into town, or, as in *Unforgiven*, riding into Big Whiskey from his isolated ranch far out of town.

On the practical filmmaking level, this Italian and Hollywood background has meant that Clint has learned to work on smaller budgets to imaginative and striking effect, combining both influences in an unusual form of artistic schizophrenia. And Bummy, in the nine films he has done for Clint, has succeeded magnificently in giving shape to Eastwood's cinematic visions. As I have discussed earlier, Bumstead's long studio years making so many westerns, half on location, half at the studio, have given him an instinctive feel for the genre. Added to this talent, Bummy's ability to work with small budgets, like that of *I Married a Monster from Outer Space*, and very short production schedules has also served him well, for he can efficiently and effectively get difficult and demanding jobs done on time and often ahead of time while staying under budget. It is hard to imagine a more perfect matching of talents than Eastwood as director/actor and Bumstead with his vast experience and ability to deliver a "look" that Eastwood has always been very pleased with. Thus if the Eastwood western

Bummy (center) with Clint Eastwood and Kevin Spacey on the set of
Midnight in the Garden of Good and Evil. *Photo by Sam Emerson.*
Copyright © 1997 by Warner Bros. Courtesy of Henry Bumstead.

is often about the lone individual on a horse, that singular figure is well
supported by Bummy and his team shading that narrative down to the last
detail of location, set, and atmosphere.

*There must be an overall pleasure in working on Eastwood's films since you
have done nine of them. What is that pleasure?*
Bumstead: It has been a learning experience and a pleasure working on all
of Clint's films I have done. Clint does his homework, so it's fun to work
with him. It's not one of those films where everyone from the script girl
on up gives opinions as to where to put the camera. Clint knows where
it should be, so no time is wasted.
*What was your first film with Clint as actor that you worked on, and what
were your impressions of those first contacts?*
Bumstead: *Joe Kidd* for Universal was the first time I met Eastwood. John
Sturges directed, and he's a top director. In fact, he had done one of
my favorite films, *Bad Day at Black Rock.* We shot in the High Sierras
near Lone Pine, and I created a little Mexican village high in the hills,
church and all. I liked Clint immediately. I remember it was very cold.
We had to heat the paint to brush it on. Then we moved to Tucson, Ari-

zona, and the old Tucson set. Believe it or not, we had snow one day, but we had built sets in a convention center, so we didn't have to shut down. We built a big courthouse, exterior and interior, that I was proud of. We ran out of money, so they wouldn't let me put a roof on it. The rains came, and it was a mess trying to get our scenes. Also the script had never solved the problem of how to get Clint into town. They finally came up with the scene in which Clint comes in on a train that runs past the station and into a saloon! At the last minute we had to bring a crew from Hollywood and move the train station and run tracks on in to the saloon with breakaway walls, a hundred yards away. It worked beautifully, thanks to my construction crew. As I remember, there was a similar scene in a TV show years later. And who knows, maybe we weren't the first to do this!

PAINTING THE WHOLE TOWN RED:
HIGH PLAINS DRIFTER
High Plains Drifter (1973); *directed by Clint Eastwood; produced by Malpaso (Robert Daley) for Universal; written by Ernest Tidyman; cinematography by Bruce Surtees. Cast: Clint Eastwood, Verna Bloom, Marianna Hill, Mitchell Ryan, and Jack Ging.*

The perfect partnership of Bumstead and Eastwood is evident from start to finish in *High Plains Drifter*. The film is, for starters, one of the very few westerns I can remember that is set in a town by a large mountain lake. *High Plains Drifter* is a tale of the lone rider (Eastwood, with no name given in the film!) coming into an isolated town and becoming a hired killer working to help the town survive a raid by outlaws. But it is also a story of how he is carrying out his own agenda of revenge. Toward these ends, *High Plains Drifter* skillfully mixes street scenes and exteriors with a wide variety of interiors ranging from the hotel to the barbershop, the saloon, and more.

The opening and closing scenes give the film a circular structure, framed by Clint riding out of what seems like a shimmering cloud on the horizon—is he real or mythical or both?—and then coming into Lago, the town by the mountain lake. Location becomes our first attraction to this tale simply because it looks so different from those stories shot on the Texas, Oklahoma, Utah, or New Mexico plains. We are high in the mountains rather than down on the plains.

The final shoot-out in the town of Lago in High Plains Drifter.
Copyright © by Universal Pictures.

Then we arrive in town. Unlike the typical western movie town (many of which used the same sets over and over again), Lago is constructed with so many buildings, which stand separate from each other, and a number of them are in a partially finished state. Once more, western films seldom acknowledge that, in fact, real western towns were thrown up quickly and never finished, with many buildings in various stages of construction.

So many westerns take place largely in the open, out of doors. But roughly 70 percent of *High Plains Drifter* is filmed inside using a variety of sets that represent the different aspects of this isolated town. There is the barbershop where Clint kills three "hombres" while getting a cut and a shave; the saloon; the hotel, with several bedrooms; a barn where Clint has his way with one of the village women; and a few houses, complete with outhouses. Again, it's hard to remember another western that offers us so many different interiors.

Then as the plot unfolds, we realize that as the town gives Clint total authority, he becomes a dictator creating a dark carnival of effects, such as turning the local town dwarf into a sheriff and, finally, demanding that the whole town be painted red, like "hell" itself. "Welcome to Hell" is then painted across the sign for Lago. Many critics have commented on how striking this ending is, both visually and symbolically, for what is being shown in the film. William Beard remarks that "the most astonishing stroke of all comes when the unpainted wood buildings of Lago are painted at last, and in the most artificial, stylized and symbolic way" (140).

The Eastwood character within the film's narrative, therefore, becomes an "artist" himself, consciously "directing" actions, characters, and the overall dramatic effect created by those around him. And Bumstead's sets are such a clear expression of Eastwood as director of the film and as character in the narrative.

High Plains Drifter *was your first film with Clint as director.*
Bumstead: Yes, Clint had already directed *Play Misty for Me* in 1971. Clint was interested in shooting *High Plains Drifter* in Nevada, but during a scouting meeting, the Teamsters were beginning to make more and more demands, so the producer pulled the plug, and we came home to California to select another location. Clint had seen a TV show shot around Mono Lake in the High Sierras that has marvelous calcium formations. So I watched one of the TV series, and I told him the series had the action too far from the lake. That's why we built the set so close to the lake. We flew up there, and Clint liked the location when we got close to the lake. So I came home and designed the set with helpful advice from Bruce Surtees, the cinematographer.[2] It was a rush job because we had to start filming on a certain date, and the head of construction at Universal said we could never build the set by that date, but we built and dressed it in twenty-eight days!

How did we do it? We took four of our best foremen and gave each a fourth of the street to build. And then they had a race to see who could finish first. It was great. We lived in Lee Vining [the nearest town] and would start at six A.M. each morning and work to two or three P.M. After that, many of the crew would go trout fishing!

We were to shoot on a Monday, and the Sunday before, the key people on my crew were sitting on the porch of the hotel. The set was all finished and dressed, both interiors and exteriors. Clint and Bob Daley, the producer, drove down the street in a pickup. They turned around at the end of the street and passed the hotel. And they gave me the thumbs-up sign as they passed the hotel. So on Monday Clint started filming.

High Plains Drifter was the first time I saw video used: Clint would tape a shot and then go into a van and look at the video. If it looked good we would move on to the next scene. Other directors do this now, but this was the first time I had worked with a director who worked this way. I realized right then that Clint was the kind of director who did his homework and knew what he wanted in a scene.

On *High Plains Drifter* we had some wonderful shots in a very confined area. It was then that I realized Clint could shoot in the smallest places without moving walls out. We had a barbershop scene, for instance. It was a very small room, but Eastwood squeezed in and got the scenes.

We filmed the whole picture in Lee Vining. We built no sets in the studio! Remember *Paint Your Wagon*, that musical Clint was in that was shot up in Oregon? Clint told me they wasted so much money building a set in a distant location and flying actors in and out by helicopter. It was crazy, he said, and of course he was right. Clint made up his mind there that if he ever directed a film, he wouldn't waste money like that, and he hasn't!

Was it an automatic decision on both of your parts to work together again?
Bumstead: Well, after *High Plains Drifter*, Clint's producer, Bob Daley, said that Clint loved the way I worked, and would I go with his company full time? But I was still working with George Roy Hill and Hitchcock, and I wanted to do more films with them. Then in 1982 Clint sent me the script of *Honky Tonk Man* and wanted me to work with him again. I don't remember what happened, but I was busy at Universal and had to turn it down.

UNFORGIVEN: "WE BUILT THE WHOLE STREET — EXTERIORS AND INTERIORS — IN FORTY-THREE DAYS"

Unforgiven (1992); directed and produced by Clint Eastwood; written by David Webb Peoples; cinematography by Jack N. Green. Cast: Clint Eastwood, Morgan Freeman, Gene Hackman, Richard Harris, Jalmaz Woolvett, Saul Robinek, Frances Fisher, and Anna Thompson.

Bumstead received an Academy Award nomination for his work on *Unforgiven*. But he was not the only one: nominations also went to the film for Best Picture; Eastwood for acting, directing, and producing; Jack Green for cinematography; David Webb Peoples for the script; Joel Cox for editing; Gene Hackman for best supporting actor; and the sound crew for best sound. And Oscars were won for Best Picture, Best Director (Clint Eastwood), Best Editing (Joel Cox), and Best Supporting Actor (Gene Hackman).

Bumstead deserved the Oscar for *Unforgiven*, for he created a whole western town from scratch in Calgary, Canada, in forty-three days, the fastest job he can remember ever completing besides *High Plains Drifter*, and despite the obvious obstacles of working almost literally in the "middle of nowhere" without the backup support of the studios' shops and personnel.

The whole production was in the same spirit, for, as Richard Schickel explains in his fine documentary on the making of *Unforgiven*, Clint kept all automobiles off the set to keep a pristine silence, and the complete film was shot in fifty-five days, weeks ahead of what most Hollywood films require. As Clint says in the documentary, "We purposely chose a spot with no civilization where we could make 360-degree shots."

David Peoples's script is rich in mixtures of familiar western characters and stories, not to mention a knowing wink to Eastwood's previous roles as a "rebellious maverick" (P. Smith 77), but it is turned inside out and upside down as well so that the film becomes both a summation and critique of all of Eastwood's career in westerns. Here he is the aging gunfighter trying to be a family man who tries to win some money for his two motherless children by taking on a just cause—the punishment of a man who cut up some prostitutes in a faraway town. Coming as the film did at this point in Eastwood's career and America's own post-Vietnam era, critics have also pointed to how important a film *Unforgiven* is in opening up and examining various shades of what is meant by "masculinity." As Dennis Bing-

Clint on his hog farm in Unforgiven *with Bumstead's attention to the detail of rough bricks in the walls. Copyright © 1992 by Warner Bros. Inc.*

ham comments, "Eastwood's persona was based on a realization that the foundations of masculine identity had been lost and needed to be massively reconstructed and re-performed" (174). Thus the telling confusion and mystery around his previous roles of a Man with No Name and in *Unforgiven* as a character with a last name of "Munny," which sounds very close to "money."

We do not have to go further into a psychocultural analysis, but once more, as in films such as *High Plains Drifter*, Bumstead built sets that reflect Eastwood's aging and evolving character. Bummy's sets also work well for exterior and interior scenes without the need for studio work. And the "360-degree" territory of Canada is used to give an impressive sense of space for Eastwood's hog farm, for Morgan Freeman's ranch, for Gene Hackman's ranch, which is always under construction in the film, and for the town of Big Whiskey, where the bulk of the film takes place.

The contrast and tension between wide-open exterior locations and tight interiors that characterize *High Plains Drifter* are all the more apparent in Bummy's work on *Unforgiven*. Celebrated production designer Mel Bourne (who designed many Woody Allen films, including *Annie Hall*, *Manhattan*, and *Zelig*, and others such as *The Fisher King*) identifies how important "space" is for him: "Space is my most important tool. One could say color, line, a study of materials, but they all have to do with how they're used in space" (LoBrutto 114).

Bummy's work certainly reflects a similar philosophy. Many exterior shots in *Unforgiven* give us a sense of how small and insignificant the characters are against the sweep of nature. And yet so much of the film plays out in the confined spaces of Big Whiskey, Wyoming—in the bedrooms of the house of prostitution, in the saloon where the bloody shoot-out takes place, leaving bodies everywhere, in the shed where Clint nurses his wounds, and even on Clint's hog farm, which we see near the opening of the film.

Again, Eastwood's desire to work in tight spaces pays off, as seen in the saloon shoot-out. In a traditional western gunfights would be taking place in fairly spacious drinking halls; in this one, the saloon is very simple and darkly lit, and we get to almost "feel" how rough the floor is at one moment when Clint is forced to crawl along it. All of this texture and use of space add up to a very powerful experience for the viewer. In fact, the documentary on the making of the film adds to our admiration for Eastwood and Bumstead's joint efforts. We watch Clint and his crew literally crammed into the saloon, which looks and feels so much more "real" than a studio set, which is usually constructed without a ceiling wall to aid camera crews and others in getting the scene on film efficiently.

How did you get started on this amazing project?
Bumstead: I had just returned from a location scout in Rome and Florence, Italy, with George Roy Hill and producer Bob Crawford on a film called *Winning Ugly*, about American football in Italy. Clint called and wanted me to do *Unforgiven*, which was originally called *The William Munny Killings*. I said I was waiting for word from George Roy Hill about *Winning Ugly*. As I remember, Clint said he would wait a week or two. Shortly after that, Hill contacted me to say *Winning Ugly* had been canceled, so I signed on with Clint. However, I had made a commitment to fly to Berlin for a week for a gathering of art directors from all over the world at the Academy Der Kunste. Clint said, "Go! We'll hit it when you return."

Clint, Jack Green, David Valdes, and I took the Warner jet to Calgary, Alberta, when I returned from Germany. Then we went by helicopter to scout for the location. We found a place we liked, landed, spotted the set, and returned to Burbank the same day!

On westerns, I always run the main street east and west so that you

Big Whiskey, Alberta, the complete town Bumstead constructed for Unforgiven. *Courtesy of Henry Bumstead.*

Big Whiskey under construction from the street level. Courtesy of Henry Bumstead.

Interior of the café at Big Whiskey, complete with old potbelly stove and extended stovepipe. Courtesy of Henry Bumstead.

have backlight in the morning and backlight in the afternoon. That seems to work the best because cameramen always love backlight! So I came home and started laying out the street with my assistant, Adrian Gorton, and set designer, Jim Murakami, still not knowing if we had the location. When I roughed out the plan, I called Clint. He came up to the office and liked what we had done. As I remember, I think he changed the location of one building from the original roughed-out version of the street.

So Big Whiskey was like a complete studio, in which every building was finished on the interior as well as the exterior. So that meant the buildings we didn't film in became the camera department, the props, sound, sign shop, the makeup department, and the building where we had snacks and coffee. It was a complete studio. Each building was used in some way for its interior as well as exterior, even if it was just for storage.

How far was it from anywhere?

Bumstead: Doug Wilson, my paint boss, and I stayed in Calgary. The set, Big Whiskey, was an hour and a half away from Calgary. However, the crew stayed in Brooks, three hours from Calgary, when shooting the hog

General store in Big Whiskey, exterior view. Courtesy of Henry Bumstead.

farm, and then they moved to Drumheller, an hour and a half from Calgary, for the filming of Morgan Freeman's ranch. From there, the crew moved to High River, which was half an hour from Big Whiskey. I brought only one man, Doug Wilson, my painter, from Hollywood. I would meet with him and my Canadian assistant, Rick Roberts, at six A.M. and we would drive three hours to Brooks. Then I would go out and raise hell to get the right character for Clint's hog farm.

You see, Clint always wants his "Seventh Army"—as I call the whole support team with trucks and all—within walking distance of a set, so that means I had to build Clint's hog farm set in a hollow because Clint wanted a 360-degree view. It turned out the Seventh Army was only a quarter of a mile away, just a nice walk to the set.

On the way home we would stop by Drumheller to check Morgan Freeman's ranch. By the way, many prehistoric creatures were found near Drumheller. I would add that my decorator on *The World According to Garp* was named Drumheller and was from this town, which was named after his family.

After checking the sets in Drumheller and Brooks, I would go back through Calgary and out to Big Whiskey to see how things were going there. So I did this trip three or four times a week. When we finished at night, it was always about ten-thirty or eleven P.M., we'd have a bite to eat and turn in. Then we would get up at five-thirty the next morning! Yes, I was a little younger then, only seventy-five!

Actually we found out the property had at one time been Crown property belonging to Edward VIII. He had visited it three or four times, and when he came, they brought a lot of Scotch and had a great time. So part of Edward's old ranch house is still there. We had to build a road four miles in to the street, which I include in the forty-three days we spent building the set. It was rough work, very rough on my back!

It was a real production, I mean we must have had a hundred carpenters and painters who put in all the pilings and flooring. I had framers in Calgary framing all the walls. And I had a mill there building doors, windows, etc., and all the millwork. Also I had another group building trusses for the buildings. So meanwhile we were painting thousands of shingles, and I brought out regular house shingle layers from Calgary to put them on, so that is why we were able to build Big Whiskey in forty-three days! It was a great operation.

Of course it was a difficult job. Doug Wilson, my Los Angeles painter and the only man I brought from Hollywood, quit almost every other day because the Canadian painters were not film painters and didn't know anything about aging the set. However, they learned and did a good job. Believe it or not, most were women.

Clint started filming the hog farm in Brooks, then out at Morgan Freeman's ranch in Drumheller. As I have said, the set was a complete city, so if the weather got bad, we just moved inside and shot scenes! But then we had a big snow, and that's when Clint filmed the shed where Clint's character was recovering from his wounds. While it snowed, he filmed toward the snow and when the snow melted, he filmed toward the interior of the shed. That's what Clint did so well. He could add what wasn't in the script. He just seized the opportunity, and that scene added beauty to the film.

We started out shooting all night—which is murder for the cast and crew. As I remember, Gene Hackman said he wouldn't have taken the role if he had known there would be that much work at night!

It was then that we started to do half nights, half days. The company would start at eleven A.M. and finish at eleven P.M. On one Sunday we

Interior of Clint's farmhouse in Unforgiven. *Courtesy of Henry Bumstead.*

had a call at ten-thirty A.M. The wind was blowing and it was cold. And we received word that a big storm—a "chinook"—was coming. So the crew filmed straight till six A.M. and finished the Big Whiskey scenes. It was then they decided to finish filming in Sonora, California. We picked Sonora because they have a period train there that we could use for the period train sequence.

The company took two weeks off, but not me. I went to Sonora to find new locations and do what was needed to finish the film. We had built the bunkhouse in Canada, but we shipped it to Sonora, log by log!

One of the many original touches in the setup of the town is having the pros-titutes in a hotel that is actually outside the main part of town. Was that location chosen because of the script or was it your idea?

Bumstead: That was my idea. I laid out the whole town and the relation-ship of building to building in it. I must add I had a fine Canadian crew:

Rick Roberts was art director, Janice Blackie-Goodine was set decorator, Jan Kobylka was construction coordinator, and Bruce Robertson was the construction foreman.

It's a dark picture in many ways, but Clint Eastwood doesn't like moonlit nights, so there are some very dark scenes. If it's around the campfire, he wants only light from the campfire. That's his theory. Night is night for Clint, and I think that is good.

Was the set saved after the shoot? You would think a whole western town would be something to preserve!

Bumstead: No. Nothing survived, and much was stolen, even though there was at the time some talk of trying to save it.

Kevin Costner (left) and Clint on location in Texas for A Perfect World. *Copyright © 1993 by Warner Bros. Courtesy of Henry Bumstead.*

"I LOVE WORKING IN TEXAS": A PERFECT WORLD

A Perfect World (1993); *directed by Clint Eastwood; produced by David Valdes and Mark Johnson for Malpaso Films; written by John Lee Hancock; cinematography by Jack N. Green. Cast: Kevin Costner, Clint Eastwood, Laura Dern, T. J. Lowther, Keith Szarabajka, and Lee Burmester.*

One of the last credits on the screen for *A Perfect World* announces that it was completely shot in and around Austin, Texas. Clearly Bumstead and his art director, Jack Taylor, and his decorator, Alan Hicks, have gained a lot of experience working in Texas. Bummy had worked on many old westerns that used Texas, and he had worked on sets for *The Stars Fell on Henrietta* (1995), which Eastwood produced but did not direct or star in. Instead, Robert Duvall headed up the cast, directed by James Keach in an oil-well period drama. *Variety* in its review made a point of singling out Bummy's work, noting "Bumstead's evocative production design" (McCarthy 24), which included old wooden oil derricks.

A Perfect World is an unusual Eastwood film that holds up well. At the heart of this tale, set shortly before John F. Kennedy was to visit Dallas for that fateful parade in 1963, is an unusual "father-son" relationship between an escaped con—Kevin Costner—and the young boy (T. J. Lowther) he kidnaps for his futile road journey through the backroads of East Texas.

The best scenes are the interaction between Costner as a kind of father figure and this boy, who has no real father. And Eastwood himself plays the smaller role of an aging sheriff out to find him in a "high-tech" trailer van with other law enforcement "experts" assigned to him by the governor. Like *Unforgiven*, this film was also shot completely on location.

Bumstead is truly that rare production designer who has been able to work on studio films that were almost completely done on the lot—including, as we have noted, *To Kill a Mockingbird* and *The Sting*. And yet he has been equally talented at making real locations work for him and the films being shot "out there." A lot of *A Perfect World* is shot in fields and outside lonely Texas farmhouses. But Bumstead also managed to find Martindale, a perfect small town, where he added buildings, signs, and did set dressing for the film. He created a general store in an empty building and built a set—interiors and exteriors—for a poor family's home. He also redesigned an actual trailer to be the high-tech trailer van that Eastwood occupies for most of his role. In the opening scenes, Bummy makes use of a real prison in Huntsville for the escape sequence. Of course, in contrast to *Unforgiven*, the film did not require Bumstead to build an entire town from scratch— a bonus!

One set that Bumstead and his team built inside a building in Martindale was the whorehouse where Costner kills the man who has been bothering the boy's mother. Bummy explains that Eastwood was delighted with the set and commented, "Bummy, you sure knew how to build a whorehouse for this film, and in *Unforgiven* and other films. Where did you get all your experience?" Of course this comment had the whole crew in stitches, but not Lena, Bumstead's wife, who was there at that moment!

Nothing was particularly difficult on the shoot, but it was rushed, as usual. Most all of Eastwood's films have been rushed simply because he likes to work swiftly and on a tight and short schedule. One surprise, however, for those who have seen the film is that the cornfield scenes between Costner and the boy were mostly shot on a "cornfield on the stage." Bumstead constructed it in a building in Austin that the crew used as a sound stage. "We brought in a lot of corn," Bummy comments. The long shots of the field, of course, were made on location. But all the close-up work was done inside!

You've done a lot with Clint, including A Perfect World, *shot in Texas. Do you like working in Texas?*

Dennis Haysbert (left) as a secret service agent in Washington with an on-location interior for Absolute Power. *Photo by Graham Kuhn. Copyright © 1997 by Castle Rock Entertainment.*

Bumstead: I love working in Texas. Yes, I've done all of Clint's films since *Unforgiven*, except for *The Bridges of Madison County*. I was working on *The Stars Fell on Henrietta* when Clint was doing *The Bridges*. Leonard Maltin, by the way, singles out my sets for *Henrietta*, calling them a real labor of love from the people at Malpaso: cinematographer Bruce Surtees and production designer Henry Bumstead! I remember, for instance, that for *Henrietta* we had to build six or seven old wooden oil derricks. That was a job!

What do you love about working in Texas?

Bumstead: I like Texas, especially Austin. Every direction is a different look, and that's important. Most of all I love the people! You see, I had worked in Texas long before working with Clint, but I used to hate the Texans, for they were such braggarts. We used to say, do you know how we find Texas if we are coming from California? And the answer is you go east until you can smell it and south until you step in it. And then you are in Texas! But I have a lot of good friends there, and Tom Copeland, head of the Texas Film Commission, and his staff are always a great help. Kate McCarley, our location manager, was a wonderful help, too.

Then in *Absolute Power* we did a lot of exteriors and interiors in Baltimore and some parts in Washington, D.C. That was a tough show. We built a lot of sets in Baltimore and Washington, D.C., but also in the Warner Brothers studio. In Baltimore I found this Catholic school that worked perfectly for the millionaire's home. However, we did have lots of construction and set dressing to do there. The main thing I remember is that when filming started at home, Clint gained eighteen days on

Alison Eastwood and John Cusack on location in Savannah for Midnight in the Garden of Good and Evil. *Photo by Sam Emerson. Copyright © 1997 by Warner Bros.*

the shooting schedule. He's that way, *fast.* He would do a four-day shoot in two! We were going nuts, working days and nights trying to get ahead of him. But we did, and I think it's a good film.

Midnight in the Garden of Good and Evil (1997) throws us into a world completely different from that of the American West and Northwest. Suddenly Bummy was working to capture the decadence of the Old South crossed with murder in Savannah, as reflected in John Berendt's popular novel.

This was clearly a stretch for Eastwood to direct and a real challenge for Bumstead: to work both on location in Savannah and to re-create much of the interior at the Warner Brothers studio, such as Jim Williams's courtroom, jail, and morgue as well as Kevin Spacey's mansion. I was able to visit the set as he finished the study, complete with paintings, furniture, and much decoration. You really did feel you were in an old Savannah home.

You spent a number of weeks on location in Savannah. Was it difficult to work there?

Bumstead: Well, at the time I was doing *Home Alone 3* in Chicago. It was zero degrees there, and I would leave on Friday afternoon and go to Savannah where the temperature was in the eighties and scout locations. Then I would fly back to Chicago on Sunday afternoon and it was still zero! All that traveling was tough on an old man like me, but I was the only one of the few on *Home Alone 3* who didn't get a cold.

We worked *so fast* on *Midnight* that I had two decorators—Dick Goddard and John Anderson. Anderson was in Savannah and Goddard in Hollywood. In the Williams house, we had to empty the real antiques, replace them with our antiques, and then return the real ones after filming. It was a big job but an enjoyable one, and my decorators did a wonderful job.

True Crime (1999) was, Bummy claims, one of the easiest pictures he ever did. Designing for a gripping story of an aging reporter in the San Francisco area trying to salvage his life at the end of his career as he investigates a condemned prisoner at San Quentin, Bumstead had to work with newsrooms and prisons.

Why was this one such an easy film for you?
Bumstead: It just was. Everything clicked: the locations, the sets we built on location in Oakland, everything worked, just like a hot knife going through butter! I am quite proud of the newsroom we built in a building that also had our offices. We shot some scenes at San Quentin, but most of the other prison interiors I built in an airplane hangar at the Alameda Air Station, which was closed.

"CLINT, WAIT, THERE'S MORE!": SPACE COWBOYS
Space Cowboys (2000); *directed and produced by Clint Eastwood for
Malpaso Productions; written by Ken Kaufman and Howard Klausner;
cinematography by Jack N. Green. Cast: Clint Eastwood, Tommy Lee Jones,
Donald Sutherland, James Garner, James Cromwell, Marcia Gay Harden,
William Devane, Loren Dean, and Courtney B. Vance.*

Certainly one of Clint Eastwood's strongest qualities is his sense of humor. And nowhere in his long career is this more apparent than in *Space Cowboys*. Assembled together is a marvelous over-the-hill gang of aging actors—Clint, Donald Sutherland, James Garner, and Tommy Lee Jones—who are able to laugh at themselves, each other, and finally accept growing older as they head into space one more time on a mission of national importance to inspect an old Russian satellite.

Eastwood as actor and director embodies both elements of classical Hollywood storytelling—strong story lines, clear characters, and final resolution to each story—as well as certain postmodern tendencies and attitudes (Beard 11). Just the title—*Space Cowboys*—clues us in to the fun Eastwood has in store for us. "An amiable yarn," says Leonard Maltin (1028), and it is obvious that everyone had fun working on this far-fetched plot, which asks us to believe that the Russian satellite is so old that only old-time Army Air Force flyers of that vintage would be able to defuse it.

For Bumstead, production design involved far more work in coming up with spaceships and outer space than he could ever have dreamed of when working on *I Married a Monster from Outer Space*. In fact, *Space Cowboys* brought together the new edge of production work—computer graphics and special effects—and the world of set and production design as Bumstead has always practiced it. In addition to using many locations in and around Los Angeles, he created the flight deck and the mid deck of the space shuttle, constructing them on the shell of an actual old Russian flight deck that was rented.

Space Cowboys *is an unusual blend of your sets and computer graphics from Industrial Light and Magic, which has done digital animation for so many big films in recent years. Could you say something about how you combined both?*

Bumstead: The moment I got the script, we began to do research. My art director, Jack Taylor, and I began gathering all the information he could find on the space shuttle. And I brought in a team of outstanding set designers. Jack and I went out and looked for all the locations mentioned in the script with Kokayi Ampah, our location manager. This all has to be done before we can make an estimate on how much sets will cost, and of course making a budget is always important.

So we got all the information we could on the shuttle, and we rented a flight deck that needed lots of work. You see, at this early point we were not getting any help from NASA because they were waiting for the approval from the Defense Department. Finally we did get NASA support, which would have helped us a lot more if we could have begun with it, but it all worked out well.

Also don't forget we had to research Russian satellites, too—Joe

The birthday card given to Bumstead on Space Cowboys. *Courtesy of Henry Bumstead.*

Musso, a talented illustrator, worked on that. He did something like a hundred and fifty sketches of the space sequences. Then we went up to Northern California and met with Michael Owens and his staff from Industrial Light and Magic. Michael was in charge of our project. At that conference we put all of our sketches on the wall in their conference room and spent a couple of days discussing them. Clint drove up from Carmel to ILM headquarters in San Rafael. And we went over all the sketches with him. He was very pleased.

How involved was Clint in that meeting?

Bumstead: Well, he looked at everything and made a few changes and

Bumstead's elaborate and accurate set for the Mission Control Center on Space Cowboys. *Courtesy of Henry Bumstead.*

seemed happy with our display. Then I told Michael Owens we would clean up the drawings, but Owens shocked me by saying, "We'll take it from here." And what he meant was that he and his team were able to employ "animatics," using computer graphics and making VCR tapes that they sent to Clint, complete with digital "characters" and sets.

Space Cowboys *is your seventh Clint Eastwood film. Was it different from any of the others—from* Unforgiven *to* Midnight in the Garden of Good and Evil?

Bumstead: Every picture is different with Clint. But when you work with Clint, it's almost like the old studio system because, as I've said, he uses his same team basically, including cinematographer, assistant director, costume designer, film editor, and others. So it makes working conditions enjoyable.

For this film, Clint hired me and my assistant, Jack Taylor, on November 30, 1998. And I hired Joe Musso, because I knew there was going to be a lot of sketching and storyboarding. So that was my team at the time. Later in 1998 when we got the script, knowing the film was a "go," we set up our art department. We didn't start filming until July 19, 1999, so we had time to do our complicated drawings and to get our sets ready. To have all this prep time for an Eastwood film was very unusual. Thank goodness, we had time to design the whole production. It's actually the longest time I ever had on a film: six and a half months, and, believe me, we needed every bit of it, even with a wonderful team of set designers.

I was in touch with you throughout your work on Space Cowboys *and enjoyed hearing how all was progressing. But in retrospect what was the most enjoyable part of working on the film?*

Bumstead: It was a tough show. The best part, however, was learning all about the space program. We were in Houston at the Johnson Space Center and Cape Kennedy. And we were meeting and talking with real astronauts and seeing the environment they lived and worked in.

How much of Space Cowboys *was shot on location?*

Bumstead: Not very much. I would say it was shot half on location and half on the stage. I didn't go for the filming at the Johnson Space Center in Houston or the Kennedy Space Center because I was too busy at the studio. However, I did have someone representing me. I did make several trips to Houston, though, to get information on our NASA sets.

I don't think I saw Clint more than three or four hours before we started filming. He trusts me, so it's fun to work with him, just as it was for George Roy Hill. They each gave me a lot of freedom.

Was there actually a model for the Russian satellite?

Bumstead: We gave ILM our drawings, and they sent us their drawings. After many exchanges they built a model, and we built a set. And of course we didn't always see eye to eye. But in a real sense, ILM has an advantage because they can say, "We can save money if we do it this way or that," and I can't deny that. Peter Rubin was in charge of the animatics crew and they were very good. The whole end "tag" on the moon, for instance, was done by ILM. You see, originally, we were going to build a moon set, but after talking it over, that was one example of something ILM did to save money. They did a fantastic job.

When we started filming the flight deck, we had a real astronaut, Bob Cabana, come to check the sets. He couldn't believe how authentic they were. He had commanded four space flights, so he knew what he was talking about. Furthermore, when Cabana heard I had worked on *The Bridges at Toko-Ri*, he threw his arms around me and said he had seen that film ten or twelve times and it made him want to be a navy flyer. So I guess I influenced his life. That made me feel good! But the flight deck and the mid deck were difficult technical sets to make at my age, so I was lucky to have such good help.

I had a wonderful designer, Jim Murakami, working on the Russian satellite. It was a very difficult job. When it was all over, I told Michael Owens that if we ever did another picture together, he would have to have one of his men working with us. That way, we would know what ILM was doing, so there would be no confusion. In several cases, they made big changes without our knowing it. Thus we had to redraw the satellite to adjust to what ILM had done.

And that Russian satellite was very complicated to build and dress. When I get on a picture now, I have my own team: Jack Taylor, art director; Lynn Price or Mike Muscarella, construction coordinator; Dick Goddard, set decorator; and Doug Wilson or Kirk Hansen, paint foreman.

Then we got busy on the local locations. It was difficult, for instance, to find Clint's suburban house. But we finally found one in Castaic, California, not too far from Piru. But the problem was that the house would take a day and a half to shoot, and the second half of that second day had to be used to shoot the church scene with James Garner. So we had to find a church nearby Clint's home in order to meet the schedule. And we did succeed in finding a church near Piru.

Jack Green, who is a great cinematographer, was almost the last person to show up on the film. I had worked with him on *Unforgiven* and every Eastwood picture since then. He's great to work with. Then I photographed and mounted pictures of all our locations, and it was near time to start shooting.

Clint came in at that point to look at the locations. And Clint says, "It looks good, Bummy," after seeing only about a quarter of our locations, and starts to leave! I grabbed him and said, "Clint, wait, there's more," and everyone laughed. And he did stay and look at a few more.

We filmed at March Field outside of Riverside, California. That's where they have a Blackbird SR-71, the plane that can fly from Los Angeles to New York in an hour and a half. That's the scene where Tommy Lee Jones tells about his cancer.

Where was the early scene of the joyride with Tommy Lee Jones?

Bumstead: That was at Agua Dulce Air Park in Agua Dulce, California. The café was in that area too.

A practical question: do you negotiate your own salary each time or do you go through an agent?

Bumstead: No, I have an agent who handles all of that.

I liked your Mission Control Center sets at the Johnson Space Center, which seemed so real.

Bumstead: We built Mission Control, a set, here at Warner Brothers, but only after visiting Houston several times and taking a lot of pictures because I wanted an exact match. It was a difficult picture to do, but with all the talented help everything went smooth as silk. We did the shooting in sixty-two days! Two months. And Clint did something else he's never done before: I don't think we ever started before ten A.M.! So you would work six hours, eat, and then work till eight or nine P.M. This was great because it meant we could come in at six A.M. if we had things to do and get things done before Clint arrived.

So when you were working on the sets, did you ever get final approval from NASA or were you just looking for input?

Bumstead: Yes, we did get NASA's approval after the Department of Defense okayed us. But I never did get to see a real space shuttle. Clint went inside one, but we just used our research. And we designed and built the airplane in the opening sequence, the X2. It was a single-seater and we had to make it a two-seater. We also needed to add ejection seats, so that was a lot of technical drawing. Our team did wonderful drawings for this, and also ILM made a model from our drawing in the opening sequence that they used. ILM was flabbergasted when they received our drawings. They were beautiful!

The astronaut who came to your set was there to check it out for accuracy?

Bumstead: Yes and no. I think Clint just wanted him around for a few days while we were filming to be sure the scenes with the flight deck were accurate. Oh, and I must say, we shot a number of days at the Boeing plant in Lakewood, California. They were so cooperative and helpful. Their rooms, etc., were a big contribution to our film.

When the picture ended, did you save any of the sets—for instance, the satellite?

Bumstead: No, saving sets is too expensive these days because storage space is at a premium. The satellite was expensive—about $350,000—and it was destroyed. After all, who would want a Russian satellite? The flight deck and the mid deck were sent back to our rentals in 100 percent better shape than they were when we brought them over!

If Clint calls tomorrow for a new project, is the answer yes?

Bumstead: [big smile] It really depends on my health. If I can get my crew that I usually work with, I would consider it because I love working on films with Clint and my talented crew.

SIX

Final Takes on a Handful of Favorites

The "etc." principle is the assumption we tend to make that to see a few members of a series is to see them all.
E. H. GOMBRICH, Art and Illusion

Production designer Patrizia von Brandenstein (*Breaking Away, Amadeus*, etc.) conveys one of the deep pleasures of the field: "One of the attractive things about this business of production design is the opportunity to become an expert on a lot of different subjects in a very short time" (LoBrutto 182). My study of Henry Bumstead's wide-ranging contribution to Hollywood art direction and production design closes with a look at a handful of films that stand out in his mind because of the directors he worked with or the special challenges of the project or both. We could easily have listed a dozen favorites beyond those already covered in previous chapters, but after much discussion, we shortened the list to the following as both diverse and representative of "enjoyable" projects that might otherwise be overlooked: Nicholas Ray's *Run for Cover*, Billy Wilder's remake of *Front Page*, John Cornell's *Almost an Angel*, Sidney Poitier's *Ghost Dad*, Paul Newman's *Harry and Son*, and Martin Scorsese's remake of *Cape Fear*.

A sketch for the saloon in Run for Cover *exhibiting Bumstead's fine control of light and shadow. Courtesy of Henry Bumstead.*

NICHOLAS RAY'S *RUN FOR COVER*:
A WESTERN WITH A DIFFERENCE

Run for Cover *(1955); directed by Nicholas Ray; produced by William H. Pine for Paramount; written by William C. Thomas from a story by Harriet Frank Jr. and Irving Ravitch; cinematography by Daniel Fapp. Cast: James Cagney, Viveca Lindfors, John Derek, Jean Hersholt, and Ernest Borgnine.*

Nicholas Ray became something of a legend for getting memorable performances out of actors whose limits we thought we knew. In a mixture of genres and styles ranging from *Born to Be Bad* (1951) and *The Lusty Men* (1954) to James Dean in *Rebel without a Cause* (1956) and *55 Days at Peking* (1963), Ray gave life to his famous line, "If it were all in the script, why make the film?" But also important was his vision of America. According to David Thomson, Ray understood that "self sufficiency and free-for-all in American life have made for alienation and violence" (615).

In short, Ray was able to give a memorable edge to story and script material that might otherwise seem quite placid and predictable. This is certainly true of his work with the western in *Run for Cover*. Even the title sounds like a typical western. But in Ray's hands, a most unusual tale of a drifter (James Cagney) who winds up becoming sheriff of a small western town after being accused of being a train robber, emerges, together with a complex "father-son" narrative as Cagney tries to befriend and mentor a young drifter (John Derek), who not only rebuffs such generosity but takes advantage of Cagney's friendship and even tries to kill him off by the film's end. Woven in with all of these narrative strands is a romance with a Swedish immigrant (Viveca Lindfors), a nod to the kind of ethnic diversity that was part of the original West.

For Bumstead's talented eye, *Run for Cover* again provided the opportunity for working both on location in Colorado and New Mexico and at the studio to play exteriors of landscape and distance against the interiors of a small town as well as caves in Aztec Ruins National Monument in Aztec, New Mexico. There is also the simple Swedish immigrant's farmhouse. In fact, it would be a very interesting Bumstead triple feature to see *Run for Cover, High Plains Drifter,* and *Unforgiven* back to back because they all show his touch for capturing a "period" sense of the West in small details, ranging from the woodwork to wallpaper, from hand-painted signs to the sense of a town as an odd collection of individual buildings hurriedly thrown up without "city planning." Add to all of this an interesting footnote: Nicholas Ray started his studies in architecture with Frank Lloyd Wright!

Run for Cover *was one of your favorites, another western, this time directed by Nicholas Ray. What was so special for you about this one?*

Bumstead: First of all, it was fun to work with Ray, who was then and even more so now a "cult director." And I liked working with James Cagney, who starred in it. He was a very nice man, not at all cocky, as he appears in many of his films. We shot it way up in the Colorado mountains, above Durango in Silverton.

I took a street in Silverton—not the main street but a secondary one—and I worked it all over so that it met the requirements for our script: a period western. Plus I built the exterior of a church there and finished the interior of the entrance so that we could shoot a few scenes looking out on the street as actors entered. That standard "trick" one learns early in one's career.

So we ended with about 70 percent of the film being shot at the studio and 30 percent on location.

You've worked with so many different directors who did westerns. So is someone like Nicholas Ray very different in what he wants out of a western than, say, Clint Eastwood?

A kitchen sketch for the immigrants' ranch in Run for Cover.
Courtesy of Henry Bumstead.

Bumstead: It's pretty hard to compare anyone to Clint, and I'll tell you why. It's that Clint works so fast and he knows exactly where to put the camera. He surprises me all the time that way. Nicholas Ray was very good, but more conventional as a director, even if his stories may have been a bit different.

But in another way they are the same: they come to the project knowing the script so well and what they want out of it.

WILD ABOUT WILDER: *THE FRONT PAGE*
The Front Page *(1974); directed by Billy Wilder; produced by Paul Monash for Universal Studios; written by Billy Wilder and I. A. L. Diamond; cinematography by Jordan Cronenweth. Cast: Walter Matthau, Jack Lemmon, Susan Sarandon, David Wayne, Carol Burnett, Austin Pendleton, and Charles Durning.*

Billy Wilder, originally of Vienna, was paid the ultimate tribute when, shortly before his death, critic Andrew Sarris called him "probably the greatest living director" (*Billy Wilder: The Human Comedy*). From

Double Indemnity (1944), *Lost Weekend* (1945), and *Sunset Boulevard* (1950) to *The Seven Year Itch* (1950), *Some Like It Hot* (1959), and *Irma La Douce* (1963), Wilder, with the help of screenwriter I. A. L. Diamond, fashioned stylish dramas and comedies that show no signs of aging.

The year 1974 was late in Wilder's career, but there is no sign of a slacking of his talent in this playful refashioning of the classic 1931 comedy of the same name, directed by Lewis Milestone from Ben Hecht's dark comedy about the newspaper business and a public hanging about to take place in Chicago. Of course, Wilder had assembled a brilliant cast—Jack Lemmon, Walter Matthau, Susan Sarandon, and a bevy of character actors. But an equal amount of credit should go to Bumstead and the richly detailed sets representing Chicago in 1929. Coincidentally, Bummy is working in the same zone—Chicago in the 1920s—on *The Sting*, for which he won the Oscar the year before.

The Wilder-Bumstead pleasures begin immediately with an imaginative credit sequence that details every aspect of newspaper printing, from the laying of type into the type frame to the actual paper coming off the press. Bumstead's efforts are thus clear from the beginning, for even before a word is spoken we feel the times, we "get" the location, and we also understand our subject matter: the press and how it is a business run on deadlines and involving a whole chain of workers.

The main sets are the pressrooms, including one wood-paneled room, the pressroom, used for the poker game being played by the reporters, and the editor's office, with its glass windows looking out onto the wide newsroom filled with activity, desks, reporters, lights, old phones, and noise. There is also the large and richly ornate movie palace, filmed on location in Los Angeles. The fiancée (Susan Sarandon) of star reporter Hildy (Jack Lemmon) plays the grand organ there. Furthermore, each set is full of period props, from old telephones on the reporters' desks to the old photographs on the walls of several offices. Brightly lit, as comedy most always is, *The Front Page* plays not as a remake so much as a vibrant, fresh satire of American media, city politics, and the crossfire of both as they deal with capital punishment.

The sets for The Front Page, *like those for* The Sting *one year before, are period Chicago sets. Was it fairly easy, therefore, to come up with 1929 Chicago?*

Bumstead's set for The Front Page, *designed to capture the clutter of a busy city newspaper office. Copyright © by Universal Pictures.*

Bumstead: Yes, I enjoyed working with Billy Wilder a lot because he is so talented, so thorough, so organized, so professional. But, yes, it was a Chicago film again, and we did build it mostly on the lot except for a few locations, such as the old movie theater that was in downtown Los Angeles. What was unusual about the pressroom is that we built the whole set—stairs, corridors, offices, etc.—on a platform. When the characters go upstairs and down into other rooms of the newspaper building, they are actually walking into rooms that were upstairs or downstairs on the set! So the editor didn't have to make a cut from the first floor to the second. So when they look out the window at the gallows, they are actually looking out the window and seeing our set for the gallows down below!

I was very happy that when I showed drawings and sketches to Wilder, he showed them to his cowriter I. A. L. Diamond, and Diamond said, "Great!"—so Wilder was pleased.

Did you watch the original The Front Page *before working on the film?*

Bumstead: No, I didn't.

The opening montage showing the whole process of putting together and printing a paper before we see any of the characters was clever, but it wasn't in the original film. Was it in the script from the beginning?

Bumstead: It does give the flavor of a newspaper of that day, doesn't it? And, yes, it was in the script. As I remember, we may have used an old newspaper printing building in South Pasadena, but Wilder was pleased, and it does look very good, doesn't it?

And we shot all the exterior car chase street scenes in the old part of downtown Los Angeles.

You chose this as one of your favorites that we haven't discussed. Could you say more?

Bumstead: I watched it again recently, and it is very funny! And what a cast. They were all marvelous, but I must say, I had just completed *The Great Waldo Pepper* with George Roy Hill when I went to work on *The Front Page*, and I think that was Susan Sarandon's first real break. So it was a surprise that when I walked on the set, Susan ran over and gave me a hug and a kiss as if I were an old friend. Billy Wilder was surprised too, of course! I'll never forget it!

GHOSTS ANGELIC AND FATHERLY:
ALMOST AN ANGEL AND *GHOST DAD*

Ghosts, especially serious ones, appear to have taken over what seems like half the films coming out of Hollywood in recent years. But two projects Bummy enjoyed working on deal with offbeat comic ghosts. They are *Almost an Angel*, starring Australian actor Paul Hogan, and Bill Cosby in *Ghost Dad*, both set in California and made in 1990. And both make use of the tried-and-true formula of a middle-aged man who has made past mistakes in his relationships and now has a chance to help others and set things straight. Redemption with humor and some special effects—that is the name of this game that Bumstead had to "bring to life."

Both ghost stories are contemporary, and both made use of Southern California for locations. But as always, Bumstead tailored homes and other environments to meet the character of the particular protagonist.

Bumstead wanted the set to look "normal" for Ghost Dad.
Copyright © 1990 by Universal City Studios, Inc.

Almost an Angel *(1990); directed by John Cornell; produced by Paul Hogan and John Cornell for Paramount; written by Paul Hogan; cinematography by Russell Boyd. Cast: Paul Hogan, Elias Koteas, Linda Kozlowski, Doreen Lang, Douglas Seale, Robert Sutton, and Travis Venable.*

Ghost Dad *(1990); directed by Sidney Poitier; produced by Terry Nelson for Universal; written by Chris Reese, Brent Maddocks, and S. S. Wilson; cinematography by Andrew Laszlo. Cast: Bill Cosby, Kimberly Russell, Denise Nicholas, Ian Bannen, Christine Ebersole, and Barry Corbin.*

Ghost Dad *and* Almost an Angel *are both about ghosts. Do ghosts change the way you do production design?*

Bumstead: [laughter] No, I think a good art director can design sets for any kind of film, and I really did enjoy both of those films. *Ghost Dad*, for instance, was funny but also sad [in] that Bill Cosby was a ghost and had a hard time dealing with his family. And when he gets in bed with the beautiful female neighbor, he falls through the bed! But I think we did well with the sets and special effects. We shot most of *Ghost Dad* on the lot, with some location work in South Pasadena, and shot the

The "ordinary" transformed in Ghost Dad. *Photo by Howard Bingham.*
Copyright © *1990 by Universal City Studios Inc.*

Priest Douglas Seale comforts ghost Paul Hogan in a chapel set by Bumstead in Almost an Angel. *Copyright © 1990 by Paramount Pictures Corporation.*

opening scenes up in the mountains nearby. Sidney Poitier, a fantastic actor and a gentleman, was a marvelous director to work with. Bill Cosby was wonderful, too.

With Eastwood's films, you comment that they were always a "rushed job." What about a film like Ghost Dad?

Bumstead: That was rushed, too. I had picked locations for the house in South Pasadena and sent them back east where Poitier was working at the time because we had a tight schedule. But I am not complaining, because Poitier was easygoing and Bill Cosby as the ghost dad would tell jokes all day. It was terrific. I went up to Poitier one day with wallpaper samples since the ghost dad's house has many rooms. And he asked me, "Bummy, how long have you been in this business?" I told him over fifty years or so at that time, and he laughed as he replied, "I don't know anything about wallpapers. Why are you showing them to me?"

How was it working with Paul Hogan and his Australian group for Almost an Angel?

Bumstead: That group was marvelous. The director, John Cornell, and most of the crew were also Australian, and we filmed interior sets at Paramount here in Los Angeles and in Fillmore, California. It's funny,

I didn't think I would get the job when I went for the interview in Cornell's office at Century City. John Cornell and his staff were there, and we spoke a while and then he asked if I wanted to do the film. I said, "Yes, of course," but asked if they would be interviewing more people. Cornell replied that they had already interviewed quite a few production designers but that he wanted me because, as he said, "I looked at your credits, which are impressive, and then when you walked in the room, I looked at your hands. And I made up my mind if your fingers were not arthritic, I would hire you. So when you played with the pencil while we talked, I realized you were not arthritic!"

They were a fun crew from beginning to end. Different from a regular Hollywood group, for sure! They gave a bonus to all the crew. Plus they gave my wife and me a three-week trip to Australia, all first class. You can't beat that! We went everywhere, including the Great Barrier Reef. And I was there in Brisbane for the opening of a film school and also spoke at the film school in Sydney, a great school. I also did radio, television, and newspaper interviews. Australia is a friendly and beautiful country.

A FLORIDA DUO: PAUL NEWMAN'S *HARRY AND SON* AND MARTIN SCORSESE'S *CAPE FEAR*

These two favorites of Bumstead's projects were shot entirely in Florida. They also shared being smaller productions that had a strong personal touch because of their directors: the well-known actor turned director Paul Newman and the well-known New York City director Martin Scorsese, taking on a non-Manhattan, non-Brooklyn project.

Of course, one of the pluses of working in Florida is that the climate is more like California's than, say, New England's or Chicago's. And yet, as we shall see, there are difficulties, too. For the weather can turn from sunshine to thunderstorm and hurricane in no time at all. Also, as on any location shoot, the crew does not have the studio space and equipment needed to give life to complicated sets and scenes. Adding up the pluses and minuses, however, Bumstead still has many fond memories of each of these Florida-shot films.

Harry and Son: The Son Also Rises

Harry and Son *(1984); directed by Paul Newman; produced by Paul Newman and Ronald L. Buck for Orion; written by Ronald L. Buck and Paul Newman from the novel* The Lost King, *by Raymond DeCapite; cinematography by Donald McAlpine. Cast: Paul Newman, Robby Benson, Ellen Barkin, and Wilford Brimley.*

Harry and Son was clearly a film that Paul Newman felt he wanted to make and had to make after his own son died. The script, from a novel by Raymond DeCapite, is an intense look at a father-son relationship two years after the wife and mother has died. The arc of the story is well framed in the opening and closing shots. The film opens with Newman as the operator of a huge destruction crane that is destroying an old building, and it closes with Robby Benson peacefully sitting on the Florida beach at sunset with his old high school sweetheart and her newborn child that the couple will raise as a family. She doesn't know who the father is, but Benson has accepted her as he has accepted his now deceased father.

In many ways, the film is the reverse of Irwin Winkler's recent father-son drama, *Life as a House* (2001), in which an oddball father (Kevin Kline) who has alienated his son in the past manages to redeem himself in the eyes of his son and his ex-wife before dying of cancer, by building the house he always wanted to build. Destruction rather than construction is Harry's character in *Harry and Son* as Robby Benson tries hard to live up to his self-destructive father's impossible dreams for his son. Both films are about redemption, but it is the son who saves the father by story's end in Newman's film, as Benson becomes a published author with a promising career, a woman he loves, and a child he accepts. Having worked on several films in which Paul Newman starred, such as *The Sting* and *Slap Shot*, Bumstead enjoyed the chance to do production design for a Newman-directed project.

The sets range from the crumbling old buildings Newman is destroying in the opening scene to the simple white frame house where Harry and his son live, surrounded by an ugly industrial Florida landscape. But much of the film is location work by the ocean, on the docks, and along the streets of Fort Lauderdale. Exteriors/interiors include bars, warehouses, car washes, etc.

Central to all is the home, which has the character of the absent wife/

The single and struggling father (Paul Newman) speaking with his loyal son
(Robby Benson) on their low-income Florida porch in Harry and Son.
Copyright © 1984 by Orion Pictures Corporation.

mother. The simple dignity and good taste of this working-class home suggest a spirit of decency that is missing in the lives of Harry and his son.

How did you connect with this project? Did Paul Newman come to you since you had worked with him on some of the George Roy Hill films?

Bumstead: Yes, Paul called for me, and I went with him to Florida to scout more locations, because he had already been down there doing some work. He had chosen a house for the story, but I had to build the interiors in an old warehouse there. The whole thing was fun to work on because Paul Newman is such a nice guy. He's very bright and has a great sense of humor.

How much of Harry and Son *was shot in Florida?*

Bumstead: All of it! Right there in Fort Lauderdale, Florida, which is where I did *Cape Fear* as well. And we lived on a barge that had two apartments. You know, we only worked five days a week on *Harry and Son*! So on the weekends we traveled around Florida or even the Bahamas. It was just fantastic.

I like working with Paul. I had worked with him on *The Secret War of Harry Frigg* (1968), *Slap Shot* (1977), and *The Sting* (1973). *Harry Frigg* was an enjoyable film, and I made some wonderful sets.

For an on-location project like Harry and Son, *do you bring others with you from Hollywood?*

Bumstead: I brought one draftsman with me, Henry Larrecq. He's a marvelous designer and draftsman. The drawings just roll out! He's so fast. But he never wants to have anything to do with directors and such, and he works eight to five and quits. That's it! He worked with me on *The Sting,* and I would come back after talking to George Roy Hill about some possible changes, but if it was after five when I got back to the office, Henry was gone! We worked together on many pictures, and just this year he turned ninety-one. A very good man indeed and an excellent draftsman.

Was Harry and Son *trouble-free?*

Bumstead: Well, actually we had a problem. The producer said I was spending too much on set decorating, so he went down to a rental house and rented furniture for the set without consulting with me. And I told him, "Nobody rents furniture without checking with me," and walked off. Of course, Newman supported me and told me to forget it, but there was some tension in the air. Other than that, the production went well, and Paul gave me a putter that I still use!

"Bummy, This Is One Hell of a Set":
Martin Scorsese's *Cape Fear*

Cape Fear *(1991); directed by Martin Scorsese; produced by Tribeca for Universal; written by James Webb and Wesley Strick from the novel by John D. MacDonald; cinematography by Freddie Francis. Cast: Robert De Niro, Nick Nolte, Jessica Lange, Juliette Lewis, Joe Don Baker, Robert Mitchum, Gregory Peck.*

Martin Scorsese has carved a memorable page in American film history because of the strongly character-centered films he has created in a variety of genres. And his characters are usually quite complex and often psychologically troubled. As Alain Mason notes, "In terms of characterization, Scorsese's heroes come out of a novel by Dostoyevsky: they are prone to anything crazy" (327).

Part of the pleasure of *Cape Fear* is the fact that it is so clearly a remake of the 1962 black-and-white original with some of the same cast, especially Robert Mitchum and Gregory Peck. Thus for the production designer, as for everyone else on the project and in the audience, a clearly identified remake "forces us to read in a different way, by considering its relationship to the earlier film" (Horton and McDougal 2).

You hadn't worked with Martin Scorsese before. How did this film come about for you?

Bumstead: My agent called me and said Scorsese was going to do a remake of *Cape Fear* and would I be interested? So my question was like yours: sure, I'm interested, but why does he want me? You know, he's a "New York" director, and I would assume he would get one of his New York art directors to do it. But he admired my work and said he wanted me. I asked my agent, Ray Gosnell, if he wanted to interview me, and he said, "No!" So that was it!

Did you do any homework by seeing some of his films?

Bumstead: I had seen and admired many of his films. *Goodfellas* was out then, and I saw that, which made me very nervous. He shoots 360-degree shots in almost every set, and that means a lot of work for a pro-

Juliette Lewis (left), Jessica Lange (center), and Nick Nolte in the family home that Bumstead worked hard to make "Southern" in Martin Scorsese's remake of Cape Fear.

duction designer. But that's the only film I looked at during that time before working for him. What really made me nervous was how much he moves the camera, so from my perspective I was thinking, "I am going to need 360-degree sets all over the place, and what a lot of work that will be!"

Why Florida instead of the Carolinas?

Bumstead: Scorsese's wife at the time and the producer of the film, Barbara de Fina, chose Fort Lauderdale, so Florida it was! The original version of *Cape Fear* (1962) was done in the studio and in South Carolina, which is, of course, the real South. But as you know, Florida isn't anything like South Carolina.

So I went down to Florida and began scouting locations. After a week or so, Marty sent word that he wanted to meet with me at the Breakers in Palm Beach, a marvelous old hotel, to discuss the film and look as some of the locations. I explained to him that Fort Lauderdale isn't what we think of as the "real South," but I told him I would do my best to make it look like the South. And that's what we did. We found a women's prison outside of Fort Lauderdale, for instance, and an old police station and other locations.

Marty was great to work for, but we did get some interference from the production office, which said I was overbuilding and thus overspending. So I took my drawings and showed them to Marty, who said he needed everything I had drawn. Well, having been in the business as long as I have, I figured I would end this problem right then. We had a meeting with everyone, including the talented cinematographer Freddy Francis, and we went over all of my sets, and there was no trouble after that!

So you found a location for the house belonging to Nick Nolte and Jessica Lange?

Bumstead: Yes, we found a house near the airport, but, boy, did we change the interior and the exterior! We added new stairs, lots of shutters, wallpapers, and paint, we hung moss up in all the trees, and we worked around all the noise from the airport, which wasn't easy. There was some beautiful set dressing by our decorator, Alan Hicks from New York. By the end it did look like South Carolina.

Was Scorsese any different as a director than others you have worked with?

Bumstead: Once we started filming, I discovered that Marty directs from a video monitor in another room! He would set up a scene and then go into another room to see how it looked on video. Also, he has a wonderful assistant, Joe Reidy, whom he has worked with before, but sometimes I was not getting exactly the right information. So I told Joe that I needed to see Marty each morning before we began filming to show him what I was doing with future sets. But that would mean going to his trailer around seven A.M. and meeting with him and his producer and their little white poodle they loved so much. And that was fine, because I got everything from the horse's mouth before starting the day.

One important set is the high school auditorium where De Niro meets up with Nolte and Lange's teenage daughter, played by Juliette Lewis. Where did you film that sequence?

Bumstead: We made the rounds looking for a place and found a junior college. And Marty said, "Let's see the basement," and I explained, "This is Florida, and there are no basements!" He then said, "We can't shoot here." But I said, "Of course we can shoot here, Marty," and made a little drawing, right there on the spot to show him how we could make a second-floor corridor look like a basement corridor by narrowing the corridor, lowering the height, and putting all the ceiling junk above. Well, he agreed, and we did it all on a weekend. So it was very funny when the students and faculty came on Monday and got out of the elevator— they looked pretty confused! They didn't know where they were or what had happened. Finally we built the little drama set where De Niro and Lewis meet, and it all went well. Quite a good sexy scene, isn't it?

Who else was part of your team?

Bumstead: Alan Hicks from New York was my decorator. The film was a big rush, and I did not have a set decorator, but I knew about Alan and brought him down to Fort Lauderdale. I was afraid he wouldn't do the job because it was so rushed and there are no property houses in Florida. But he worked seven days a week, and he did a marvelous job. We wound up working together on several other projects, too. It wasn't easy. But he took over immediately and drove all over Florida finding whatever we needed!

What about the final storm scenes on the houseboat and in the lagoon?

Bumstead: Well, someone had found a real lagoon and swamp that was near the ocean. But thank God we never shot there, for it would have been impossible due to all the elements: tide, wind, and rain. We would still be there shooting if we had tried to do the houseboat scenes there.

So Freddie Frances and I went to Marty and the producers and said we would have to build a tank on a stage to do the scenes, and they seemed horrified. The problem was that Marty didn't want to go to California or to Universal Studios in Orlando, Florida, where tanks and stages existed. Also there wasn't anything available when we wanted to shoot, anyway. That's when I said that we would have to build a huge stage that would include a tank for the houseboat and a 360-degree backing that would resist rain, wind, etc. And we would have to start building it immediately to keep on schedule. It was a very big job supervising the construction of the stage, taking care of the company and the other sets. But somehow we did it and everything worked out well.

I'm actually very proud of the set we built, because we had a 360-degree backing, painted by local artists, which could resist wind and rain to create the scenes required in the script. We built five different houseboats, each one for a different scene. When De Niro and Marty entered the stage and walked onto the houseboat that was in the water and ready for filming, De Niro looked around and said, "Bummy, this is one hell of a set." Marty smiled and said, "Ya! Ya! Ya!"

Scorsese really enjoyed the set. As you see in the film, we had wind and rain coming from fire hoses all over the place, and Marty would come in wearing boots, rehearse, then go inside his plastic hut and watch it on the monitor. He was like a kid with a new toy, for he had

Juliette Lewis, Jessica Lange, and Nick Nolte struggle to survive in the storm scene of Cape Fear. *Copyright © 1991 by Universal City Studios, Inc., and Amblin Entertainment, Inc.*

never done this kind of thing before. You know, so much of his work in New York was filming on actual locations.

I don't think he had ever done matte shots or worked with a gimbal [which created the pitching motion of the houseboat], but he thoroughly enjoyed these new tools.

Scorsese is a real film historian as well as a director. Did that come through in his directing in any way?

Bumstead: Marty is an encyclopedia of film. He has seen everything, and I do mean everything. For instance, we would be out scouting locations and I'd mention a film I'd worked on, and Marty would immediately tell me the director, the cast, the year it was made, and everything. I also respect the fact that he does so much for film preservation.

I've heard you say there was a problem with the miniature boats used for the storm sequence. What was the problem?

Bumstead: The problem with water is scale. Water is always water: you can't make it smaller or larger. Thus I feel miniature models shouldn't be smaller than one-third of the real object's normal size or they look fake. Well, they finally decided to go with one-fourth size. I guess they were saving money, and it doesn't look too bad. Maybe just not as good as one-third would have been. Most people probably never noticed, but of course professionals would.

Any special memories in using locations for sets on this film?

Bumstead: There was the time when we were doing De Niro's room in a cheap boardinghouse, which was for the scene where he beats up the woman. The building we used was very, very sleazy. I mean, really sleazy! So I said to my assistant, "Let's add a bathroom with a pull chain toilet to give it some character."

Marty came at seven A.M. the next morning and I showed him everything, including the little pull chain toilet, which I told him was a good period detail for the set. And Marty said, "Ya! Ya!" as always. When I got back to the office a half hour later, Barbara de Fina, the producer, had called Jack [Taylor], my art director, saying that I was spending too much money and overdesigning.

But when Marty shot the scene, as you remember, he did lots of filming around the toilet. De Niro even hangs upside down on a bar in the jamb of the door to the toilet. So I felt good, because I always try to add those period details that make a difference. It was always the same with George Roy Hill, too!

Toward a Conclusion

*I would be willing to bet that few people [who] allow
a film crew to use their property, agree a second time.*
C. S. TASHIRO, Pretty Pictures

*I never was a big drinker, I didn't smoke, and didn't gamble
my money away. I guess that's why I'm still around.*
HENRY BUMSTEAD

---

*A*s I completed my interviews for this study during the fall
of 2001, Bummy was invited to speak at the Los Angeles
Film School. I was fortunate to be able to join him on that
balmy autumn afternoon, not long after the tragic events
of September 11. Almost a hundred students joined him
in a large auditorium as he showed 35mm footage from *Vertigo, Space Cowboys,* and *Absolute Power,* speaking informally about each and answering
questions from those present.

It was a pleasure for me to watch the students catching on to both
Bummy and everything he represents: a shining career that spans both
the Hollywood studio system at its best and the new Hollywood since the
1960s with its emphasis on "freelance" and location shoots. Clearly students wanted more after the two hours zoomed to a finish. Many came up
afterward with questions that he fielded with interest and clarity. I feel the
students did realize how lucky they were to be in touch with so much of
Hollywood and its history through the work of one vibrant artistic director
and production designer.

On the way home that day, we were given a ride by a student in his midthirties who had a wife and children and who had now decided to become
a filmmaker. He talked to Bummy about the "thesis" film he would shoot
for the school, and ended with this comment: "Mr. Bumstead, I want you
to know that before I heard your talk this afternoon, I was not sure if my
film should be shot on location or on a set. I now know I want to build a

set! Thank you!" Bummy smiled and added: "There's nothing wrong with locations either, you know!"

I have touched only a few of the highlights here of the richly lived life of Henry Bumstead within the studios of Hollywood and on vastly different locations around the world. Future studies, however, will surely further illuminate the importance of production design to the fabric and meaning of cinema in general and each film in particular. But clearly the name Henry Bumstead deserves to be in the pantheon of those great production artists who have helped turn screenplays and dreams into realities that could be filmed.

As this project drew to a close, I addressed three simple questions to Bummy before pressing "stop" on the tape recorder.

Among the group of filmmakers that you've never worked with, which one interests you most?

Bumstead: That's simple: David Lean. I enjoyed all of his films very much, including *Brief Encounter, Great Expectations, The Bridge on the River Kwai, Lawrence of Arabia, Dr. Zhivago,* and *A Passage to India!* All great films.

If you were to give your advice for young art directors and production designers, what would it be?

Bumstead: My first piece of advice would be to repeat what you've heard me say: try to do sets that look like the characters that live in them. Don't try to do all the tricks you know! If your character is a simple man, make a simple set. Don't overelaborate.

My second piece of advice would be to pay close attention to color, because color, too, should reflect the characters and the times. And my third remark would be about attention to details. I'm a freak for details on a set, and aging. Good aging is an art, and I can't stand to see sets aged badly. In my opinion, that alone is one of the main things wrong with sets today. I see badly aged fireplaces, fireboxes, walls, and woodwork. I tell students to take pictures of signs of all types, amateur and professional, because they represent a period, and it seems we are always doing streets. And signs are so important. However, I must say, I see lots of wonderful sets, too, on TV and in the theater.

Finally, if you could take aside the young Henry Bumstead who was starting out in 1937 and speak with him now, what would you tell him?

Bumstead: I really don't think I would have done anything differently. It

Bummy on the sunken ship set of Blood Work, *April 2002.*
Courtesy of Henry Bumstead.

Birthday cartoon of Bummy and Clint Eastwood, 1993. Courtesy of Henry Bumstead.

has been a fantastic life. The thing is, movies open up all areas of seeing things. You know, when I went to Paris, I saw things other people didn't see. You work on a missile film, and you are in a silo under the ground learning things, or you do a Washington, D.C., picture, and film opens doors that the average person would never be able to open. All because of the movies. I love movies!

I got to go on set with Bummy one more time before this work went to press. It was April 2002, and Bummy was hard at work on Clint Eastwood's *Blood Work* at Warner Brothers, based on the psychological police thriller by Michael Connelly.

Eastwood plays a retired FBI agent named McCaleb in California who has recently had a heart transplant. Early on, he learns that his new heart belonged to the murdered sister of a woman who looks up McCaleb to tell him the murderer was never found. McCaleb thus comes out of retirement to find the murderer who killed the woman whose heart is keeping him alive.

Bummy wanted me to see the interior of an old ship abandoned off the

California coast. As we walked onto the set at Warner Brothers on a Saturday afternoon, painters, set decorators, and assistants called out, "Hello, Bummy!" There is no other way to describe the response that Bummy generates from his team on the set than as loving respect and dedication.

We were told that we had just missed Eastwood by half an hour, but that he was totally satisfied with the look of the set. "It has to look like an old ship about to sink," Bummy explained. He then went on to say that they had been shooting earlier in the week on an actual old wreck of a ship off the California coast, which they did finally sink at sea as part of a shot. The set was thus a copy of the real ship, full of rusty pipes, peeling paint, and slanted floors. There was the smell of fresh paint, the sound of nails being driven in, and calls across the set from various decorators as they worked to make the wreck look even more weathered, tarnished, abandoned. Everything looked like old metal, but Bummy was quick to remind me, "All of this is wood, you know, just shaped and worked to look like old metal."

We drove back to San Marino that afternoon, talking not of *Blood Work* but of Bummy's next film after *Blood Work*, which he was already beginning to plan out.

I had a smile on my face that I don't think Bummy saw. "Retirement" would never be a word that such an artist of the old school from Hollywood would ever understand. Bummy is a pro who loves movies, his work making them, and the people he has worked with over the years. Could any artist ask for more?

Notes

Introduction. "Not Everything You Draw Shows Up in the Shot!"

1. Clint Eastwood to the University of Oklahoma Film and Video Studies Program, October 28, 1999, commenting on the Lifetime Achievement Award that was presented to Henry Bumstead in a ceremony at the university in November.

1. The Paramount Years: "We All Wore Suits and Ties"

1. Roland Anderson became best known for his collaboration with Cecil De Mille on such productions as *Cleopatra* (1934), *The Plainsman* (1936), *The Buccaneer* (1938), *Union Pacific* (1939), and *Reap the Wild Wind* (1942), which won an Oscar for special effects. In the 1940s "Anderson worked in a wider variety of genres, displaying a talent for modern, urban American settings" (Stephens 16).

2. Hal Wallis (1898–1986) was, according to David Thomson, "tough, smart, a tremendous manager, and a man of unshakeable self confidence" (787). He won the Irving Thalberg Award twice and could, as Thomson notes, claim to have worked at the top of his form for longer than any other well known Hollywood producer. Add to this Bumstead's comment: "He was one of the best. Even his office was amazing. It was a real producer's office. I mean, the door would automatically lock when you walked in. You don't find producers like that any more."

3. Backings are what you see through a window on a set in the background.

4. James Wong Howe (1899–1976) worked from 1917 to 1975. His films included *Prisoner of Zenda* (1937), *Abe Lincoln in Illinois* (1940), *Yankee Doodle Dandy* (1942), *The Time of Your Life* (1948), *Picnic* (1955), and *The Sweet Smell of Success* (1957) as well as *The Rose Tattoo* (1955) and *Hud* (1968), for which he won Oscars.

5. The sketches of set designs throughout this text were done by Bumstead's illustrators or sketch artists on each project, under his supervision and based on his initial rough sketches. He says he no longer has any of his own sketches from his early days as an art director. The sketch artists and illustrators for this book were Dale Hennessy, Gene Johnson, Ken Reid, Bill Major, and Tom Wright.

2. The Hitchcock Films: "Never in My Wildest Dreams!"

1. Burks was director of photography on *Strangers on a Train* (1951), *I Confess* (1953), *Dial "M" for Murder* (1954), *Rear Window* (1954), *To Catch a Thief*

(1955), *The Trouble with Harry* (1955), *The Man Who Knew Too Much* (1956), *The Wrong Man* (1956), *Vertigo* (1958), *North by Northwest* (1959), *The Birds* (1963), and *Marnie* (1964).

2. It was the same church: Ambrose Chapel (Spoto 276).

3. "Forced perspective" is "a technique used to give the illusion of depth: background elements that are supposed to look very distant are rendered in even more diminished scale while foreground elements are in full scale" (Ettedgui 204).

3. Universal Studios, Robert Mulligan, and *To Kill a Mockingbird*

1. Producer Robert Arthur was basically a Universal Studios producer who by the time Bumstead met him had made his name, with such hits as *Abbott and Costello Meet Frankenstein* (1948), *The Big Heat* (1953), and *Man of a Thousand Faces* (1957). Bumstead went on to work with him on several other projects, including *Come September* (1961), *Father Goose* (1964), and *One More Train to Rob* (1971).

2. The impostor as a young boy was played by Bob Crawford, who later became a producer for George Roy Hill.

3. Alan Pakula became a director in his own right, doing such films as *The Sterile Cuckoo* (1969), *Klute* (1972), *All the President's Men* (1976), and *Sophie's Choice* (1982).

4. Working with George Roy Hill: From Dresden to Venice and Everywhere in Between

1. Frank Tallman died in a stunt crash when he was caught in a big storm.

2. Newman, speaking to the female owner of the hockey team, says: "You know, your oldest kid looks like a fag to me, and you better get married again 'cuz he'll have somebody's cock in his mouth before you can say jackrabbit."

5. The Eastwood Films: "Clint Does His Homework"

1. Thomson goes on to describe Eastwood as an authentic hero image of our times. He "is our knight," says Thomson, "and he shames the astrologers, the alchemists, the courtesans, and the robber barons who otherwise rule the court" (221).

2. Bruce Surtees is the son of Robert Surtees, whom Bumstead also worked with. Bruce has shot a variety of Eastwood films, including *The Beguiled* (1971), *Play Misty for Me* (1971), *Dirty Harry* (1972), *Tightrope* (1984), and *The Stars Fell on Henrietta* (1995). But he has shot memorable films for others too, such as *Beverly Hills Cop* (1984), *Movie Movie* (1978), and *Men Don't Leave* (1990).

Filmography

Aaron Slick from Punkin Crick (1952), dir. Claude Binyon, Alan Young, Dinah Shore, Adele Jergens, Robert Merrill.

Absolute Power (1996), dir. Clint Eastwood, Clint Eastwood, Gene Hackman, Ed Harris, Laura Linney, Judy Davis, E. G. Marshall.

The Adventures of Nick Carter (1972, TV film), dir. Paul Krasny, Robert Conrad, Shelley Winters, Broderick Crawford.

Almost an Angel (1990), dir. John Cornell, Paul Hogan, Elias Coteas, Charlton Heston, Doreen Lang, Linda Kozwolski, Douglas Seale.

As Young As We Were (1987), dir. Bernard Girard, Robert Harland, Pippa Scott, Majel Barrett.

Banning (1967), dir. Ron Winston, Robert Wagner, Anjanette Comer, Jill St. John, Guy Stockwell, Gene Hackman.

Beau Geste (1966), dir. Douglas Heyes, Telly Savalas, Guy Stockwell, Doug McClure, Leslie Nielsen.

The Bellboy (1960), dir. Jerry Lewis, Jerry Lewis, Alex Gerry, Bob Clayton, Sonny Sands, Walter Winchell (narrator).

Blindfold (1966), dir. Philip Dunne, Rock Hudson, Claudia Cardinale, Jack Warden, Guy Stockwell.

Blood Work (2002), dir. Clint Eastwood, Clint Eastwood, Jeff Daniels, Wanda De Jesus, Tina Lifford, Paul Rodriguez, Dylan Walsh, Anjelica Huston.

The Brass Bottle (1964), dir. Harry Keller, Tony Randall, Burl Ives, Barbara Eden, Ann Doran.

The Bridges at Toko-Ri (1954), dir. Mark Robson, Grace Kelly, Fredric March, Mickey Rooney.

Bullet for a Badman (1964), dir. R. G. Springsteen, Audie Murphy, Darren McGavin, Rita Lee, Bob Steele.

Cape Fear (1991), dir. Martin Scorsese, Robert De Niro, Nick Nolte, Jessica Lange, Juliette Lewis, Robert Mitchum.

Cinderfella (1960), dir. Frank Tashlin, Jerry Lewis, Ed Wynn, Judith Anderson, Anna Maria Alberghetti, Count Basie.

Come Back, Little Sheba (1952), dir. Daniel Mann, Burt Lancaster, Shirley Booth.

Come September (1961), dir. Robert Mulligan, Rock Hudson, Gina Lollobrigida, Sandra Dee, Bobby Darin.

The Concorde: Airport '79 (1979), dir. David Lowel Rich, Alain Delon, Robert Wagner, Bibi Anderson, Susan Blakely.

Dear Brat (1951), dir. William Seiter, Mona Freeman, Billy DeWolfe, Edward Arnold. (Bumstead shared art direction credit with Hal Pereira.)

Double Indemnity (1944), dir. Billy Wilder, Barbara Stanwyck, Fred McMurray. (draftsman only)

Dr. Cyclops (1940), dir. Ernest Schoedsack, Albert Dekker, Thomas Coley. (assistant only)

Family Plot (1976), dir. Alfred Hitchcock, Karen Black, Bruce Dern, Barbara Harris, William Devane.

Father Goose (1964), dir. Ralph Nelson, Cary Grant, Leslie Caron, Trevor Howard, Jack Good.

The Front Page (1974), dir. Billy Wilder, Jack Lemmon, Walter Matthau, Carol Burnet, Susan Sarandon, Charles Durning.

Funny Farm (1988), dir. George Roy Hill, Chevy Chase, Madolyn Smith, Joseph Maher, Jack Gilpin, Brad Sullivan.

The Furies (1950), dir. Anthony Mann, Barbara Stanwyck, Walter Huston, Wendell Corey.

A *Gathering of Eagles* (1963), dir. Delbert Mann, Rock Hudson, Rod Taylor, Mary Peach, Barry Sullivan, Henry Silva.

Ghost Dad (1990), dir. Sidney Portier, Bill Cosby, Kimberly Russell.

The Goldbergs (1950), dir. Walter Hart, Gertrude Berg, Philip Loeb. (retitled *Molly*)

The Great Impostor (1961), dir. Robert Mulligan, Tony Curtis, Karl Malden, Raymond Massey, Edmond O'Brien.

The Great Waldo Pepper (1975), dir. George Roy Hill, Robert Redford, Susan Sarandon, Bo Svenson, Edward Herman, Bo Brundin.

Gunpoint (1966), dir. Earl Belamy, Audie Murphy, Joan Staley, Warren Stevens, Edgar Buchanan.

The Hangman (1959), dir. Michael Curtiz, Robert Taylor, Tina Louise, Fess Parker, Jack Lord.

Harry and Son (1984), dir. Paul Newman, Paul Newman, Robby Benson, Joanne Woodward, Ellen Barkin, Morgan Freeman.

Her Alibi (1989), dir. Bruce Beresford, Tom Selleck, Paulina Porizkova, William Daniels, James Farentino.

Here Come the Waves (1944), dir. Mark Sandrich, Bing Crosby, Betty Hutton. (assistant only)

High Plains Drifter (1973), dir. Clint Eastwood, Clint Eastwood, Verna Bloom, Marianna Hill, Mitchell Ryan, Jack Ging.

Hollywood or Bust (1956), dir. Frank Tashlin, Dean Martin, Jerry Lewis, Anita Ekberg, Pat Crowley.

Home Alone 3 (1997), dir. Raja Gosnell, Alex D. Linz, Olek Krupa, Rya Kihlstadt, Lenny von Dohlen.

House Calls (1978), dir. Howard Zieff, Walter Matthau, Glenda Jackson, Art Carney, Richard Benjamin.

I Married a Monster from Outer Space (1958), dir. Gene Fowler Jr., Tom Tryon, Gloria Talbott, Ken Lynch, John Eldredge.

Joe Kidd (1972), dir. John Sturges, Clint Eastwood, Robert Duvall, John Saxon, Don Stroud, Stella Garcia.

Jumping Jacks (1952), dir. Norman Taurog, Dean Martin and Jerry Lewis, Mona Freeman, Don Defore.

Knock on Wood (1954), dir. Norman Panama, Danny Kaye, Melvin Frank, Mai Zetterling.

The Leather Saint (1956), dir. Alvin Ganzer, Paul Douglas, John Derek, Jody Lawrence, Cesar Romero, Ernest Truex.

Little Boy Lost (1953), dir. George Seaton, Bing Crosby, Claude Dauphin.

The Little Drummer Girl (1984), dir. George Roy Hill, Diane Keaton, Yorgo Yoyagis, Klaus Kinski, Sami Frey.

A Little Romance (1979), dir. George Roy Hill, Laurence Olivier, Diane Lane, Thelonious Bernard.

Louisiana Purchase (1941), dir. Irving Cummings, Vera Zorina, Bob Hope, Victor Moore. (draftsman only)

Lucy Gallant (1955), dir. Robert Parish, Charlton Heston, Jane Wyman, Thelma Ritter, William Demarest.

A Man Called Gannon (1969), dir. James Goldstone, Tony Franciosa, Michael Sarrazin, Susan Oliver.

The Man Who Knew Too Much (1956), dir. Alfred Hitchcock, James Stewart, Doris Day, Bernard Miles, Brenda De Banzie.

McCloud, Who Killed Miss U.S.A.? (1970, TV film), dir. Richard Colla, Dennis Weaver, Craig Stevens, Peter Mark Richman.

Midnight in the Garden of Good and Evil (1997), dir. Clint Eastwood, Kevin Spacey, John Cusack, Jack Thompson, The Lady Chablis.

Money from Home (1953), dir. George Marshall, Dean Martin, Jerry Lewis, Pat Cowley, Robert Strauss. (originally in 3-D)

The Movie Murderer (1970, TV film), dir. Boris Sagal, Arthur Kennedy, Warren Oates, Tom Selleck.

My Friend Irma (1949), dir. George Marshall, Dean Martin, Jerry Lewis, Marie Wilson, John Lund.

My Friend Irma Goes West (1950), dir. Hal Walker, John Lund, Marie Wilson, Dean Martin, Jerry Lewis.

My Own True Love (1949), dir. Compton Bennett, Melvyn Douglas, Phyllis Calvert. (assistant only)

Mystic River (2003), dir. Clint Eastwood, Sean Penn, Tim Robbins, Kevin Bacon, Laurence Fishburne.

No Man of Her Own (1950), dir. Mitchell Leisen, Barbara Stanwyck, John Lund.

One More Train to Rob (1971), dir. Andrew McLaglen, George Peppard, Diana Muldaur, John Vernon.

A Perfect World (1993), dir. Clint Eastwood, Kevin Costner, Clint Eastwood, Laura Dern, T. J. Lowther.

Psycho III (1986), dir. Anthony Perkins, Diana Scarwid, Anthony Perkins, Jeff Fahey, Roberta Maxwell.

Raid on Rommel (1971), dir. Henry Hathaway, Richard Burton, John Colicos, Wolfgang Preiss.

Reap the Wild Wind (1942), dir. Cecil De Mille, John Wayne, Ray Milland, Paulette Goddard, Susan Hayward. (assistant only)

The Redhead and the Cowboy (1950), dir. Leslie Fenton, Glenn Ford, Rhonda Fleming, Edmund O'Brien.

Rhubarb (1951), dir. Arthur Lubin, Ray Milland, Jan Sterling, Gene Lockhart.

Road to Bali (1952), dir. Hal Walker, Bob Hope, Bing Crosby, Dorothy Lamour. (draftsman only)

Road to Hong Kong (1962), dir. Norman Panama, Bob Hope, Bing Crosby, Dorothy Lamour, Peter Sellers, Joan Collins. (draftsman only)

Road to Morocco (1942), dir. David Butler, Bob Hope, Bing Crosby, Dorothy Lamour, Anthony Quinn, David Butler. (draftsman only)

Road to Rio (1947), dir. Norman McLeod, Bob Hope, Bing Crosby, Dorothy Lamour, Gale Sondergaard, Frank Faylen. (draftsman only)

Road to Singapore (1940), dir. Victor Schertzinger, Bob Hope, Bing Crosby, Dorothy Lamour, Charles Coburn, Jerry Colonna. (draftsman only)

Road to Zanzibar (1941), dir. Victor Scherzinger, Bob Hope, Bing Crosby, Dorothy Lamour, Una Merkel. (draftsman only)

Rollercoaster (1977), dir. James Goldstone, George Segal, Richard Widmark, Timothy Bottoms, Henry Fonda, Helen Hunt.

Run for Cover (1955), dir. Nicholas Ray, James Cagney, Viveca Lindfors, John Derek, Ernest Borgnine.

Saigon (1948), dir. Leslie Fenton, Alan Ladd, Veronica Lake.

Sailor Beware (1951), dir. Hal Walker, Dean Martin, Jerry Lewis, Corinne Calvet.

Sainted Sisters (1948), dir. William Russell, Veronica Lake, Joan Caulfield, Barry Fitzgerald.

Same Time, Next Year (1978), dir. Robert Mulligan, Ellen Burstyn, Alan Alda.

The Secret War of Harry Frigg (1968), dir. Jack Smight, Paul Newman, Sylva Koscina, Andrew Duggan, Tom Bosley.

Showdown (1973), dir. George Seaton, Dean Martin, Rock Hudson, Susan Clark.

Slap Shot (1977), dir. George Roy Hill, Paul Newman, Michael Onikean, Linda Crouse, Strother Martin, Jennifer Warren.

Slaughterhouse-Five (1972), dir. George Roy Hill, Michael Sacks, Ron Leibman, Eugene Roche, Sharon Gans.

Smokey and the Bandit II (1980), dir. Hal Needham, Burt Reynolds, Jackie Gleason, Jerry Reed, Sally Field.

Song of Surrender (1949), dir. Mitchell Leisen, Wanda Hendrix, Claude Rains, MacDonald Carey, Andrea King.

Space Cowboys (2000), dir. Clint Eastwood, Clint Eastwood, Donald Sutherland, Tommy Lee Jones, James Garner.

The Spiral Road (1962), dir. Robert Mulligan, Rock Hudson, Burl Ives, Gena Rowlands, Geoffrey Keen.

The Stars Are Singing (1953), dir. Norman Taurog, Rosemary Clooney, Anna Maria Alberghetti.

The Stars Fell on Henrietta (1995), dir. James Keach, Robert Duvall, Aidan Quinn, Frances Fisher, Brian Dennehy.

The Sting (1973), dir. George Roy Hill, Paul Newman, Robert Redford, Robert Shaw, Charles Derning, Ray Walston, Eileen Brennan. (Oscar for Bumstead)

Streets of Laredo (1949), dir. Leslie Fenton, William Holden, Mona Freeman, MacDonald Carey.

The Story of Dr. Wassell (1944), dir. Cecil De Mille, Gary Cooper, Laraine Day, Signe Hasso. (assistant art director)

Submarine Command (1951), dir. John Farrow, William Holden, Nancy Olson, William Bendix.

That Certain Feeling (1956), dir. Norman Panama, Bob Hope, Eva Marie Saint, Melvin Frank, George Sanders, Pearl Bailey, Al Capp (technical advisor).

Tell Them Willie Boy Is Here (1969), dir. Abraham Polonsky, Robert Redford, Katharine Ross, Robert Blake, Susan Clark.

A Time of Destiny (1988), dir. Gregory Nava, William Hurt, Timothy Hutton, Melissa Leo, Stockard Channing.

To Kill a Mockingbird (1962), dir. Robert Mulligan, Gregory Peck, Mary Badham, Philip Alford, John Megna, Brock Peters, Robert Duvall. (Oscar for Bumstead)

Tobruk (1967), dir. Arthur Hiller, Rock Hudson, George Peppard, Nigel Green, Guy Stockwell, Jack Watson.

Top o' the Morning (1949), dir. David Miller, Bing Crosby, Ann Blyth, Barry Fitzgerald.

Topaz (1969), dir. Alfred Hitchcock, John Forsythe, Frederick Stafford, Dany Robin, Karin Dor.

The Trap (1959), dir. Norman Panama, Richard Windmark, Lee J. Cobb, Tina Louise, Earl Holliman.

True Crime (1999), dir. Clint Eastwood, Clint Eastwood, Isaiah Washington, Denis Leary, James Woods, Lisa Gay Hamilton.

Unforgiven (1992), dir. Clint Eastwood, Clint Eastwood, Gene Hackman, Morgan Freeman, Richard Harris, Frances Fisher. (Oscar nomination for Bumstead)

Union Pacific (1939), dir. Cecil De Mille, Barbara Stanwyck, Joel McCrea. (draftsman only)

Vagabond King (1956), dir. Michael Curtiz, Kathryn Grayson, Oreste, Rita Moreno, Cedric Hardwicke.

Vertigo (1958), dir. Alfred Hitchcock, James Stewart, Kim Novak, Barbara Bel Geddes, Tom Helmore. (Oscar nomination for Bumstead)

The War Lord (1965), dir. Franklin Schaffner, Charlton Heston, Rosemary Forsyth, Richard Boone, Maurice Evans.

Warning Sign (1985), dir. Hal Barwood, Sam Waterston, Kathleen Quinlan, Yaphet Kotto.

What's So Bad about Feeling Good? (1968), dir. George Seaton, George Peppard, Mary Tyler Moore, Dom DeLuise, John McMartin.

Whispering Smith (1948), dir. Leslie Fenton, Alan Ladd, Brenda Marshall (second unit work)

Directors with Whom Bumstead Has Worked

Hal Barwood	George Roy Hill	Nicholas Ray
Compton Bennett	Alfred Hitchcock	Mark Robson
Claude Binyon	Mitchell Leisen	William Russell
David Butler	Arthur Lubin	Boris Sagal
Richard Colla	Anthony Mann	Mark Sandrich
Michael Curtiz	Daniel Mann	George Seaton
Clint Eastwood	Delbert Mann	Franklin Schaffner
Cecil De Mille	George Marshall	Martin Scorsese
John Farrow	Norman McLeod	Jack Smight
Leslie Fenton	David Miller	John Sturges
Bernard Girard	Robert Mulligan	Norman Taurog
James Goldstone	Hal Needham	Hal Walker
Walter Hart	Paul Newman	Billy Wilder
Henry Hathaway	Norman Panama	Howard Zeiff

Selected Bibliography

General and Production Design

Affron, Charles, and Mirella J. Affron. *Sets in Motion: Art Direction and Film Narrative*. New Brunswick, N.J.: Rutgers University Press, 1995.

Albrecht, Donald. *Designing Dreams: Modern Architecture in the Movies*. New York: Harper and Row, 1986.

Aronson, Arnold. *American Set Design*. New York: Theatre Communication Group, 1985.

Auiler, Dan. *Vertigo: The Making of a Hitchcock Classic*. New York: St. Martin's Press, 2000.

Barsacq, Leon. *Caligari's Cabinet and Other Grand Illusions: A History of Film Design*. Revised by Elliot Stein. New York: New York Graphic Society, 1976.

Beard, William. *Persistence of Double Vision: Essays on Clint Eastwood*. Edmonton: University of Alberta Press, 2000.

Berthome, Jean-Pierre, ed. *Alexandre Trauner: décors de cinéma*. Paris: Jade-Flammarion, 1988.

Billy Wilder: The Human Comedy. PBS American Masters special. Directed by Mel Stuart. Produced by Mel Stuart and David Yarnell for Thirteen/WNET, 1999. Documentary.

Bingham, Dennis. *Acting Male: Masculinities in the Films of James Stewart, Jack Nicholson, and Clint Eastwood*. New York: Routledge, 1994.

Bridges, Herb. *The Filming of* Gone with the Wind. New York: Mercer University, 1989.

Carick, Edward. *Designing for Films*. How to Do It Series, No. 27. Los Angeles: Studio Publications, 1941.

Corliss, Mary. "Designed for Film: The Hollywood Art Director." *Film Comment* 12, no. 2 (May/June 1978): 25–27.

Carnes, Mark C., ed. *Past Imperfect: History according to the Movies*. New York: Henry Holt, 1995.

Custen, George F. *Bio/Pics: How Hollywood Constructed Public History*. New Brunswick, N.J.: Rutgers University Press, 1992.

De Govia, Jack. "60 Years of Art Direction." In *Society of Motion Picture and Television Art Directors IA 876: 1998 Membership Directory*. Studio City, Calif., 1998.

Douy, Max, and Jacques Douy. *Décours de cinéma: les studios français de Mélèis à nous jours*. Paris: Editions du Collectionneur, 1993.

Ettedgui, Peter. *Production Design and Art Direction*. Screencraft. East Sussex, England: Rotovision, 1999.

Frankl, Paul. *Principles of Architectural History: The Four Phases of Architectural Style, 1420–1900*. Cambridge: MIT Press, 1968.

Geddes, Norman Bel. *Horizons*. 1932. Reprint, New York: Dover, 1977.

Gombrich, E. H. *Art and Illusion: A Study in the Psychology of Pictorial Representation*. Princeton: Princeton University Press, 1972.

Halliwell, Leslie. *Halliwell's Film Guide*. 19th ed. Edited by John Walker. New York: HarperPerennial, 1995.

Heisner, Beverly. *Hollywood Art: Art Direction in the Days of the Great Studios*. New York: McFarland, 1990.

———. *Production Design in the Contemporary American Film: A Critical Study of 23 Movies and Their Designers*. Jefferson, N.C.: McFarland, 1996.

Henderson, Brian. "Notes on Set Design and Cinema." *Film Quarterly* 42 (fall 1988): 17–28.

Horton, Andrew. *The Films of George Roy Hill*. New York: Columbia University Press, 1982.

———, ed. *Comedy/Cinema/Theory*. Berkeley: University of California Press, 1991.

———, and Stuart McDougal, eds. *Play It Again, Sam: Retakes on Remakes*. Berkeley: University of California Press, 1998.

Landy, Marcia. *Cinematic Uses of the Past*. Minneapolis: University of Minnesota Press, 1996.

Levy, Shawn. *King of Comedy: The Life and Art of Jerry Lewis*. New York: St. Martin's Press, 1996.

LoBrutto, Vincent, ed. *By Design: Interviews with Film Production Designers*. Westport, Conn.: Praeger, 1992.

Lourie, Eugene. *My Work in Films*. New York: Harcourt Brace Jovanovich, 1985.

Maltin, Leonard. *Leonard Maltin's 2002 Movie and Video Guide*. New York: Signet Books, 2001.

Marner, Terence St. John. *Film Design*. London: Tantivy Press, 1974.

Mason, Alain. "Martin Scorsese." In *American Directors*, edited by Jean-Pierre Coursodon, 2:326–329. New York: McGraw-Hill, 1983.

McDougal, Stuart. "The Director Who Knew Too Much: The Director Who Remade Himself." In *Play It Again, Sam: Retakes on Remakes*, edited by Andrew Horton and Stuart McDougal, 52–69. Berkeley: University of California Press, 1998.

Mitchell, Lee Clark. *Westerns: Making the Man in Fiction and Film*. Chicago: University of Chicago Press, 1996.

Naumberg, Nancy, ed. *We Make the Movies.* New York: Norton, 1937.

Neumann, Dietrich, ed. *Film Architecture: Set Designs from* Metropolis *to* Blade Runner. Munich and New York: Prestel, 1999.

Olson, Robert. *Art Direction for Film and Television.* New York: Focal, 1993.

Preston, Ward. *What an Art Director Does.* Los Angeles: Silman-James, 1994.

Sarris, Andrew, quoted on Billy Wilder in TV documentary, *Billy Wilder: The Human Comedy* (PBS, February 2001).

Schatz, Thomas. *The Genius of the System: Hollywood Filmmaking in the Studio Era.* New York: Pantheon, 1988.

Schickel, Richard. *Clint Eastwood: A Biography.* New York: Knopf, 1996.

Searles, Baird. *Epic!: History on the Big Screen.* New York; Abrams, 1990.

Sennet, Robert S. *Setting the Scene: The Great Hollywood Art Directors.* New York: Abrams, 1994.

Smith, Paul. "Eastwood Bound." In *Constructing Masculinity,* edited by Maurice Berger et al. New York: Routledge, 1995.

Smith, Ronn. *American Set Design 2.* New York: Theatre Communications Group, 1991.

Sorlin, Pierre. *The Film in History: Restaging the Past.* Totowa, N.J.: Barnes and Noble, 1980.

Spoto, Donald. *The Art of Alfred Hitchcock: Fifty Years of His Motion Pictures.* New York: Hopkinson and Blake, 1976.

Stephens, Michael L. *Art Directors in Cinema: A Worldwide Biographical Dictionary.* Jefferson, N.C.: McFarland, 1998.

Sterritt, David. *The Films of Alfred Hitchcock.* New York: Cambridge University Press, 1993.

Surowiec, Catherine. *Accent on Design: Four European Art Directors.* London: British Film Institute, 1992.

Sylbert, Paul. *Final Cut: The Making and Breaking of a Film.* New York: Seabury Press, 1998.

Tashiro, C. S. *Pretty Pictures: Production Design and the History Film.* Austin: University of Texas Press, 1998.

Thomson, David. *A Biographical Dictionary of Film.* 3rd ed. New York: Knopf, 1995.

Thompson, Kristin, and David Bordwell. *Film History: An Introduction.* New York: McGraw-Hill, 1993.

Thompson, Richard, and Tim Hunter. "Clint Eastwood." In *American Directors,* edited by Jean-Pierre Coursodon, 2:11–117. New York: McGraw-Hill, 1983.

Toplin, Robert Brent. *History by Hollywood: The Use and Abuse of the American Past.* Urbana: University of Illinois Press, 1996.

Vacche, Angela Dalle. *Cinema and Painting: How Art Is Used in Film.* Austin: University of Texas Press, 1996.

Vidler, Anthony. "The Explosion of Space: Architecture and the Filmic Imaginary." In *Film Architecture: Set Designs from* Metropolis *to* Blade Runner, edited by Dietrich Neumann, 13–25. Munich and New York: Prestel, 1999.

Wood, Robin. *Hitchcock's Films Revisited.* New York: Columbia University Press, 1989.

On Henry Bumstead

Alexander, Brandy, ed. "Tribute to Henry Bumstead." In *The Society of Motion Picture and Television Art Directors 1998 Membership Directory*, 24–27. Santa Monica, 1998.

Abbott, Denise. "Tricks of the Trade: Henry Bumstead." *Hollywood Reporter*, May 1993.

Glazier, Bill. "A Life in Film: Film Achievements of Henry Bumstead." *The Quarterly Magazine* (Huntington Library), 14, no. 1 (spring 2000): 26–31.

Horton, Andrew. "The Man with Two Oscars: Henry Bumstead." *Shot in LA*, April 1994, pp. 13–14.

———. "The World of Hollywood Art Design: An Interview with Henry Bumstead." *Cineaste* 26, no. 3 (summer 2001): 18–22.

McCarthy, Todd. Review of *The Stars Fell on Henrietta. Variety*, April 24–30, 1995, p. 24.

Troy, Carol. "Production Designer Henry Bumstead." *Premiere*, December 1991, p. 56.

Documentaries Mentioning Henry Bumstead

Crawford, Robert. *The Making of Slaughterhouse-Five.* 1972.

Engle, Harrison. *Obsessed with Vertigo.* American Movie Classics/Signal Hill Entertainment, 1997. A documentary on the restoration of *Vertigo* that includes an interview with Bumstead about his work with Hitchcock.

Kumin, Elaine, and Helen DeBolt. *Henry Bumstead: Tricks of the Trade.* The Power of Ideas. Oklahoma Scholar-Leadership Enrichment Program, University of Oklahoma. Video.

Raim, Daniel. *The Man on Lincoln's Nose: The Cinema of Robert Boyle.* Adama Films, 2000.

Schickel, Richard. *Eastwood & Co. Making* Unforgiven. Lorac/Warner Brothers, 1992. VHS.

Index